EXCEL 2022 in 7 Days

The Most Updated Course to Master Excel, Full of Practical Examples and Advanced Tips.

The Comprehensive Guide to Learn Fundamentals, Functions, Formulas and Charts Very Quickly

LEONARD WEBB

© **Copyright 2021 by Leonard Webb - All rights reserved.**

This document is geared towards providing exact and reliable information in regard to the topic and issue covered. The publication is sold with the idea that the publisher is not required to render accounting, officially permitted, or otherwise, qualified services. If advice is necessary, legal, or professional, a practiced individual in the profession should be ordered.

- From a Declaration of Principles, which was accepted and approved equally by a Committee of the American Bar Association and a Committee of Publishers and Associations. In no way is it legal to reproduce, duplicate, or transmit any part of this document in either electronic means or in printed format. Recording of this publication is strictly prohibited, and any storage of this document is not allowed unless with written permission from the publisher.

All rights reserved. The information provided herein is stated to be truthful and consistent, in that any liability, in terms of inattention or otherwise, by any usage or abuse of any policies, processes, or directions contained within is the solitary and utter responsibility of the recipient reader.

Under no circumstances will any legal responsibility or blame be held against the publisher for any reparation, damages, or monetary loss due to the information herein, either directly or indirectly. Respective authors own all copyrights not held by the publisher. The information herein is offered for informational purposes solely and is universal as so. The presentation of the information is without a contract or any type of guarantee assurance.

The trademarks that are used are without any consent, and the publication of the trademark is without permission or backing by the trademark owner. All trademarks and brands within this book are for clarifying purposes only and are owned by the owners themselves, not affiliated with this document.

TABLE OF CONTENT

Introduction 7

DAY #1 9

Chapter 1: Introduction to Microsoft Excel 10
- 1.1 What is Excel? 10
- 1.2 History of Microsoft Excel 11
- 1.3 Why Use and Learn Excel? 12
- 1.4 Examples of Using Excel 13
- 1.5 Where to download it? 14

Chapter 2: Getting started with using Microsoft Excel 15
- 2.1 What is Ribbon? 15
- 2.2 How to customize your Ribbon: 17
- 2.3 Worksheet in Excel 19
- 2.4 Row in Microsoft Excel 20
- '2.5 Column in Microsoft Excel 20
- 2.6 Other Commands on Excel Interface 23

DAY #2 25

Chapter 3: Entering, Editing and Managing Data 26
- 3.1 Concept of Cell 26
- 3.2 Enter Data in a Cell 26
- 3.3 Modifying Data in Excel 28
- 3.4 Rows and Columns 31
- 3.5 Hide or Unhide Row or Column 33
- 3.6 Insert or Delete Row or Column 33
- 3.7 Moving Column or Row 37
- 3.8 To Swap Rows and Columns 38

Chapter 4: Working with Worksheets 40
- 4.1 What is a worksheet? 40
- 4.2 Cell in Worksheet 40
- 4.3 Difference between Workbook and Worksheet 41
- 4.4 Excel Worksheet Tab 41
- 4.5 How to add a new Worksheet? 41
- 4.6 How to delete the Worksheet? 42
- 4.7 How to Copy Worksheet 43
- 4.8 How to Change Color of Worksheet 45
- 4.9 Grouping and Ungrouping of Worksheet 45
- 4.10 To Group Worksheet 46
- 4.11 Benefits of Grouping Worksheets 46
- 4.12 Ungrouping of Worksheets 46

    4.13 How to Identify Grouped Sheets 47
    4.14 Why Ungroup Worksheets? 47

DAY #3 48

Chapter 5: Sorting and Filtering Data 49
    5.1 Sorting data 49
    5.2 To sort data of a Sheet 49
    5.3 To sort data of Cell Range 51
    5.4 To Sort Data in one column 52
    5.5 To Sort Data in multiple Columns 52
    5.6 Custom Sorting 53
    5.7 To Sort Data in a Row 55
    5.8 Sorting by Conditional formatting 57
    5.9 Filtering Data 58
    5.10 How to Add Filters 61

DAY #4 69

Chapter 6: Data Validation 70
    6.1 How to Validate Data in Excel 71
    6.2 How to make a validation rule in Excel 72
    6.3 List of Excel data validations (dropdown) 72
    6.4 Copy Excel data validation rule for other cells 74
    6.5 How to remove data validation 74

Chapter 7: Formatting Cells 76
    7.1 Change the Font 76
    7.2 To adjust the font of your data 76
    7.3 To adjust the font size of your data 77
    7.4 To modify the font color 77
    7.5 Cell Alignment 78
    7.6 Adding borders and Fill colors in a cell 80
    7.7 Formatting Text and Numbers 82

DAY #5 83

Chapter 8: Formulas and Functions 84
    8.1 Formula 84
    8.2 To enter the formula 84
    8.3 To Edit Formula 85
    8.4 Make a Formula by Copy/Paste 86
    8.5 Add Formula Using Insert Function Key 89
    8.6 How to use formula? 91
    8.7 Functions 92
    8.8 Difference between Formula and Function 119

DAY #6 120

Chapter 9: Working with Excel Tables 121
9.1 What are Excel Tables? 121
9.2 Create an Excel Table.. 121
9.3 Why to Use Table 123
9.4 Excel Tables with Structured Referencing 125
9.5 Pivot Table 126
9.6 Two Dimensional pivot tables 127
9.7 Uses of Pivot Table 128
9.8 Style and Formatting of Table 129
9.9 Excel table styles 129
9.10 Table Style Options 129
9.11 Select Table Style When Creating a Table 130
9.12 Change the table style... 130
9.13 Remove table formatting 131

DAY #7 132

Chapter 10: Creating Charts 133
10.1 What are Excel Charts? 133
10.2 Types of Charts 133
10.3 Creating Chart in Excel 140
10.4 How to Create a Process- Behavior Chart in Excel 147
10.5 Creating Process- Behavior Chart 148

Chapter 11: Magical Tips for Excel 149
11.1 Paste Special 149
11.2 How to add multiple rows 149
11.3 Conditional Formatting 149
11.4 How to detect duplicate data... 150
11.5 Use Shortcut Keys 150
11.6 Copy-Paste Formulas without Changing References.................. 150
11.7 Debugging Formula 151
11.8 Need to Delete All Comments 151
11.9 Custom Sorting 152
11.10 Bullets in Excel.. 152
11.11 Multi-Level Sorting 153
11.12 Scrollable List in Excel 153

Thank you! 154

Conclusion 155

TUTORIAL: How to Create Family Monthly Budget Using Excel 156

APPENDIX 159

ABOUT THE AUTHOR

Leonard Webb was born in Phoenix, Arizona (USA) in 1982.

His passion for programming began at a young age, when he used his savings to buy one of the first computers of the time.

For over 26 years, Leonard has studied many of the technological advances the online world has to offer and spends many of his daily hours learning everything he can to make the best use of computers.

He has honed his skills as a computer programmer working for many large companies.

Since it is rare to find clear and understandable information online on the use of software, especially basic software, Leonard decided to write a series of books on the most common software, and began writing a clear and comprehensive guide on the use of Excel.

A FREE GIT FOR YOU!

To thank you for buying this book, I would like to share with you **23 fantastic Excel Templates**.

I'm sure you'll find them really useful in countless contexts.

You can get them by scanning the QR code.

Introduction

Microsoft Excel is a significant spreadsheet and data analyzing computer program with a broad range of capabilities. It has many functions to store, arrange and analyze big amounts of data. In today's world, this tool has become an essential tool across the globe for many reasons. And not having familiarity with this program can put you behind in many ways.

Every company or organization now needs this primary skill. Every educational organization, business firm, or company uses this program to collect, evaluate and organize its data. To progress, it is important to continue to learn and sharpen your skills.

According to a study by Burning Glass, 80% of job openings require spreadsheet and word processing software skills to stay competitive and up-to-date, whether you are a student, a businessman or a middle-aged man who wants to learn excel without any complexity and with a simple explanation. It is a guide that will make you solve your problem, make it painless for you to learn excel. This book will make you the master of this program. This book is a step-by-step guide for beginners, and you will become an expert of excel by the end of reading it.

Here, you will learn Microsoft Excel from zero. From where and how to download it in different devices. You will become familiar with how Microsoft Excel works. Its main features, how to enter, edit and manage data, what is a filter, and how to filter data.

This book includes making spreadsheets, making tables, setting a data validation, formulas, and creating charts. Also, its functions, number functions, text functions, logic functions, count functions, date/time functions, everything in a very simple explanatory way. You will read and design spreadsheets, edit, manipulate, sort, analyze data, and create equations by reading this book.

All the shortcuts and useful techniques are also provided to help you make the work easier for you. So, how does this book promise you that it will help you learn excel by the end? It's simple, only reading it for 7 days and you can learn excel completely. The book is divided into 7 sections, by reading each section in a day, excel can be learned within no time. Within this much, short period, you will learn excel even if you have never used it before in your life. Without waiting, keep reading it, and you will know how it will make it a much better experience for you.

As you start reading, you will realize that the information shared in this book is much easier than all those complex courses you find online, which built an intimidating stigma around it for you. But this book will make you feel better about how excel works. And the explanations in this book are very schematic and are provided with pictures and examples that will help you understand it well.

The functionality of Excel is described smoothly. That will make your work life better, improve your efficiency, productivity, and will make you better at your job. It will save you time and also will make you get more money. Who does not want that?

DAY #1

"Even the greatest was once a beginner. Don't be afraid to take that first step"

Muhammad Ali

Chapter 1: Introduction to Microsoft Excel

1.1 What is Excel?

Excel is a Microsoft Office application that many people are familiar with. Because of its spreadsheet nature, it's widely applicable. Different kinds of data can be organized, calculated and kept data saved for future use. Excel grid interface allows you to organize virtually any type of data you can think of. Excel strength rests in its ability to let you design the layout and structure of the data you wish to organize, whatever you see fit. Microsoft Excel is the highly used spreadsheet in the world.

Excel spreadsheets allow you to work with tables of numerical data organized in columns and rows that can be modified using a wide variety of arithmetic operations and functions. With Excel, you can do simple calculations, use graphing tools, and build pivot tables, macro and many other useful things. They can also show data graphs, such as bar charts, histograms, and line graphs. Microsoft excel is compatible with different operating systems that include Mac, Android, Windows and IOS.

Organizing and manipulating data is easier using Microsoft Excel, which uses rows and columns. Numbers are used to representing spreadsheet rows, whereas alphabets are given to column headers. Excel may use Visual Basic for Applications (VBA) to program in Excel, and you can use DDE (Microsoft's Dynamic Data Exchange) to retrieve data from other sources.

1.2 History of Microsoft Excel

Twenty-seven years ago, the first version of Microsoft Excel was released for Macintosh systems, while the Windows version was introduced in 1987. Following are the versions and features released of excel for windows up till now.

- Excel 1.0 was released in 1985 and is the only version released for Macintosh.
- Excel 2.0 was the first windows version released in 1987.
- Excel 3.0 was released in 1990, in which features related to the toolbar, drawing capabilities, outlining were included.
- Excel 4.0 was released in 1992 with a variety of new features.
- Excel 5.0 was introduced in 1993 and was included in Microsoft office 4.0; multi-sheet workbooks and support of VBA was the highlighted feature included in this version.
- Excel 7.0 was released in 1995 and was part of Microsoft office 95. There were few changes in this version, but it was much faster and stable than Excel 5.0.
- Excel 8.0 was released in 1997 and was part of Microsoft office in 1997. Office assistance and validation was the main feature introduced in this version.
- Excel 9.0 was released in 2000 and part of Microsoft office 2000 with a self-repair document feature.
- Excel 10.0 was released in 2002 and was part of Microsoft Office XP. The main highlighted feature in this version was identifying any error in formula and recovering spreadsheets whenever excel crashes.
- Excel 11.0, commonly known as excel 2003, was released in 2003 and part of Microsoft office 2003. The most important feature introduced in this version was improved support of XML.
- Excel 2007 was introduced in 2007. The main highlighted feature of Microsoft Excel 2007 was the introduction of the ribbon system.
- Excel 14.0 was introduced in 2010 with major updates. The improved features in this version of Microsoft excel were the inclusion of new graphic designs, improvement in a pivot table and many others.
- Excel 15.0, commonly known as Microsoft excel 2015, was released in 2015. In this version, Microsoft introduced more than 50 new features.

- Excel 2016 was released in 2016. Histogram was the new thing added in this version with many other features.
- Excel 16.0 or Excel 2019 was released in 2018 with the addition of new charts in it.
- Excel 2020 with new updates was released in 2020

1.3 Why Use and Learn Excel?

As excel is easy to use because of the ability to add and remove information without causing any difficulty, MS Excel is frequently utilized for a wide range of tasks. When it comes to anything involving financial activity, Excel is a need. Making new spreadsheets with bespoke formulae for everything from a basic quarterly forecast to an entire corporate annual report makes Excel enticing for many people. Excel is popular for organizing and monitoring common information like sales leads, project progress *reports, contact lists, and billing.

Finally, Excel comes in handy when working with huge datasets in science and statistics. Using Excel statistical formulae and graphing features, researchers may more easily do variance analysis and visualize large amounts of data. Microsoft Excel plays a vital role in so many industries. In the following departments, the importance of Microsoft Excel may be observed.

Calculations:

When it comes to conducting computations, Microsoft Excel becomes useful. Basic math, statistics, and even engineering tasks are all included in the software. Excel can handle calculations that take multiple iterations to arrive at a final solution by inserting only a few simple formula components.

Create Graphs/Charts:

Different departments can portray statistical data more visually by using Microsoft Excel various charts.

Formatting:

Excel also includes a tool for formatting cells. The cell formatting function comes in helpful when trying to figure out how things work. If a certain result is found, the cells can be structured to show that way. These are some uses that have been described above.

Microsoft Excel can conduct a wide range of functions and tasks. To this day, spreadsheets are the most effective tools for analyzing data. It's not the sole tool for handling all data tasks, but it's one of the most cost-effective and dependable options available for data analysis. Because it's built on your knowledge of the analytics process, it serves as a solid basis for generating intelligent data. For this reason, organizations continue to emphasize the significance of Excel as the most intelligent approach to obtain useful insights. Despite this, the method continues to be beneficial.

1.4 Examples of Using Excel

For regular official tasks, the Microsoft Excel program offers a broad range of functions and capabilities. Let's look at how different sorts of consumers throughout the globe utilize Microsoft Excel capabilities in their everyday lives.

- In Education Sector

Teachers might employ table layouts, forms, charts, data tools, and algorithms to instruct pupils in the classroom. Excel allows students to understand and solve fundamental and logical-mathematical issues as well as statistics. Teachers may teach students by using an Excel sheet to create a table. They may use color to highlight more attractive cells, emphasize critical numbers, and use bars and charts to illustrate data.

- In Business Sector

Does anyone believe that a business owner, whether small or large, can be effective and run their firm without using Microsoft Excel? The Microsoft Excel program is utilized in a variety of business situations. Goal-setting, budgeting, and planning, team leadership, account management, revenue and expenditure calculations, product offerings value, and client data management are all examples of commercial activities. Microsoft Excel is used in business to make everyday official processes more efficient, precise, and predictable. Excel has a lot of valuable tools, including filters, charts, conditional formatting, pivot tables, and logical and financial formulae.

- Data Analysis

Working for an internet company or website owner requires a lot of data analysis (e-commerce, blog, forums, etc.). Tracking website traffic, sales revenue, user reviews, marketing strategies, user activity, and events are just some things that are done. Such a task takes a long time and requires a lot of thought, mainly when things don't go as planned.

For online company owners and consumers, the Microsoft Excel program has a lot of advantages. Filtering users' data by nation, filtering consumers by age, applying conditional formulae to massive data, and so on are routine everyday activities with which excel can help you.

- Goals Setting and Planning

Financial, professional, and physical objectives may all be planned using Microsoft Excel. These provide you with a clear perspective of something to concentrate on while keeping you on track. These actions and tasks are accomplished by creating spreadsheets, plan papers, and logs utilizing Excel to track progress and reach the finish line.

1.5 Where to download it?

The latest version of Microsoft Excel is available on the Microsoft website and can be downloaded from there. It is the official website of Microsoft, and you can download it from here: *https://www.microsoft.com/en-ww/microsoft-365/excel*.

Buy it or try it for free and signup on the website. There are different plans and licenses available for this program. There is a license for Home and Business. See the plans and pricing of these licenses. With the Home license, there are three types of licenses. One for your usage, second for a family for 2 to 6 people, third for a student, you can only use on a single computer or laptop. The pricing is different for each one for a year. With Business one, there are four kinds of plans, i.e., Basic, Standard, Premium, and Apps for Business. Each plan has different features with different pricing for a year.

Companies mix them to get different kinds of features and improved functions according to their requirement.

Chapter 2: Getting started with using Microsoft Excel

After downloading Excel, start Excel Program. From the main window's menu, search it on the search bar and click on it. Or else double-click the excel icon. A window will pop up.

The Excel screen will appear the first time you open Excel 2021. You can create a new workbook, select a template, and access any recently edited workbooks from here. Locate and select Blank Workbook from the Excel screen to open the workbook interface. The ribbon, a strip of buttons across the top area of the program window, is essential to the Excel interface.

The ribbon is divided into tabs, each of which has a group of controls, and this nomenclature is used to indicate where tools are located. The Home tab, Type group, Bold button, for example, are used to apply a bold font to the selected range. This chapter explains the Excel interface, its ribbon, and the functions and commands available on the ribbon.

2.1 What is Ribbon?

In Microsoft excel, a ribbon is a row of tabs and icons. It is the control panel of excel. Like a quick toolbar, you can control, navigate and identify commands on it. The different icons are being grouped in nine different tabs according to their functions. Each tab has different groups of icons and commands. To help you accomplish the most frequent excel activities.

Each tab has multiple groups, and each group has multiple commands with a dialogue launcher. A dialogue launcher can be seen by clicking a small arrow at every group's lower right corner. It displays more related commands of that group.

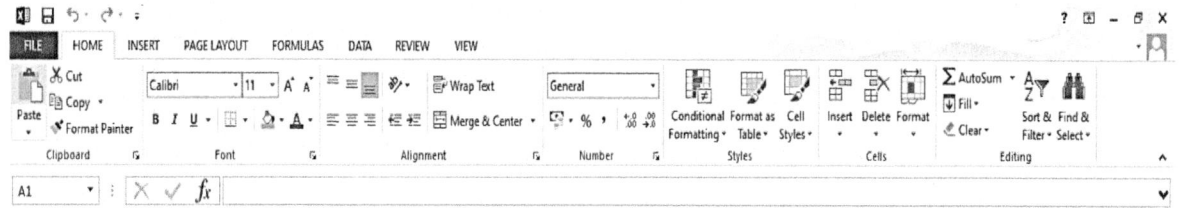

Ribbon Tabs:

Excel ribbon contains nine tabs. Which are as follows; File, Home, Insert, Page Layout, Formulas, Data, Review, View, and Help. Customized Ribbon can be made by adding new tabs having your favorite command buttons.

File: This tab permits to give access backstage view, which holds many options of excel file and customization. Includes all necessary file-related commands and settings. Excel backstage view is where you may update and manage your file data.

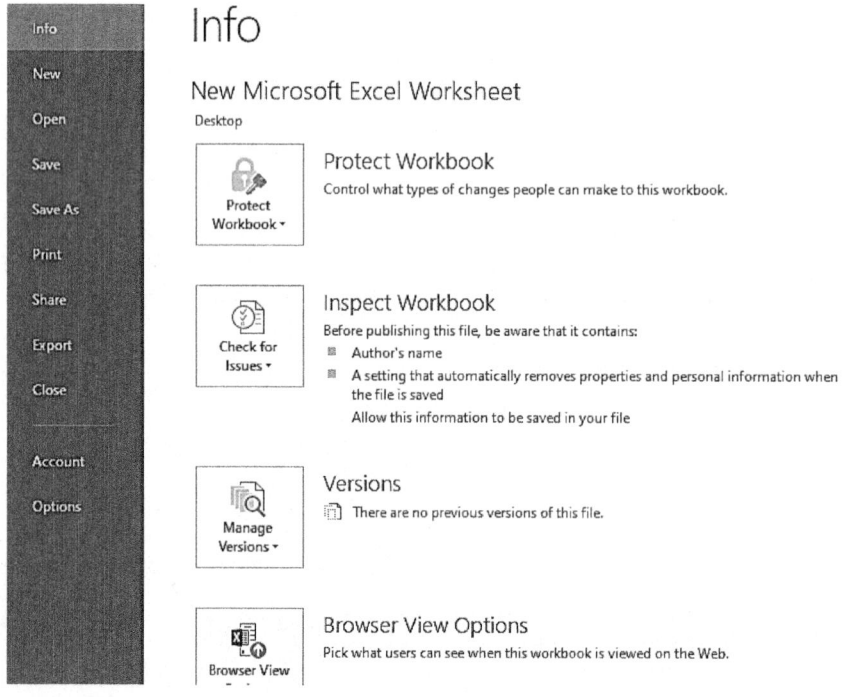

Home: This tab comprises the most commonly used commands like copying and pasting, finding and replacing, sorting, filtering, and formatting your data.

Insert: This tab is used to insert pictures, charts, tables, charts, equations, hyperlinks, icons, shapes, headers, and footers in a worksheet.

Page Layout: This tab is used primarily for page setup and printing. It manages the layout of the worksheet, its margins, alignment and print area.

Formulas: This tab provides a facility for inserting functions, naming variables, and manipulating computation parameters. It controls the calculation options.

Data: This tab contains commands for both controlling worksheet data a connecting to external data. It has options for sorting data, filtering data and manipulating data.

Review: In Excel worksheets, this tab primarily offers features for checking spells, recording changes, adding notes and comments, sharing and protecting worksheets.

View: This tab contains commands to switch between worksheets, view excel worksheets, freeze panes, organizing and managing multiple windows.

Help: Only Microsoft Excel 2019 and 365 have this feature. This tab displays the Help Task Pane, letting you contact Microsoft Support, give feedback, and view training videos quickly to help you. There is one more tab that is not visible by default in the Excel Ribbon. That is called Developer. The developer tab can be seen by clicking on the File tab, then going to options, clicking on the "Customized Ribbon," clicking on the developer option, checking its box, and clicking OK.

2.2 How to customize your Ribbon:

The Ribbon can rearrange. Click on the arrow that is in the upper right corner next to minimizing the program. A drop-down menu will open, having three options.

1. Auto-Hide Option
2. Show Tabs
3. Show tabs and Commands

Choose an option. Click on the Third option, "Show tabs and Commands," to get back the Ribbon's default view.

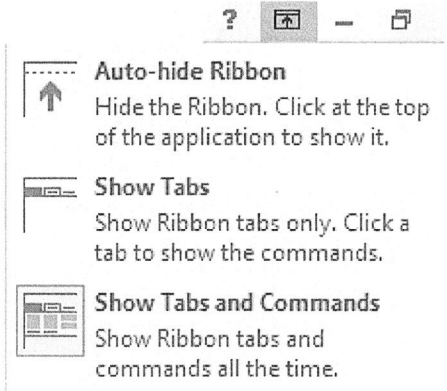

Another way to minimize the Ribbon is to right-click anywhere on Ribbon and see the option of "Collapse the Ribbon." The Ribbon will hide. To get back the commands and Ribbon default view, click on the tabs row. It will show the commands and all available buttons of these tabs, then again right-click and uncheck the "Collapse Ribbon" option.

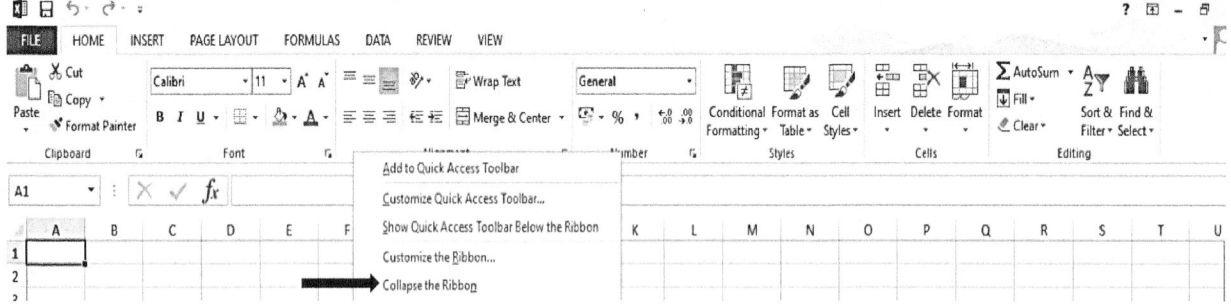

Another option that can be seen above this is the collapse Ribbon option is "Customize Ribbon". A window will pop up with a lot of options in front of you. Go to the **Main Tabs** drop-down menu and select your options. New tabs can be added, and remove existing tabs according to your choice. A new tab can add your favorite commands according to your choice, which you will use frequently. It will make your work smoother and faster.

In **the Main Tabs** drop-down menu, click on the New Tab option. Rename it, click **OK**. Now select the commands you want and add them under your group. Then confirm it by clicking **OK**. To reset Ribbon Customization, click on "Reset all Customization" at the end of the Ribbon Customization window. Excel will ask you to delete all customizations; confirm it by clicking **OK**.

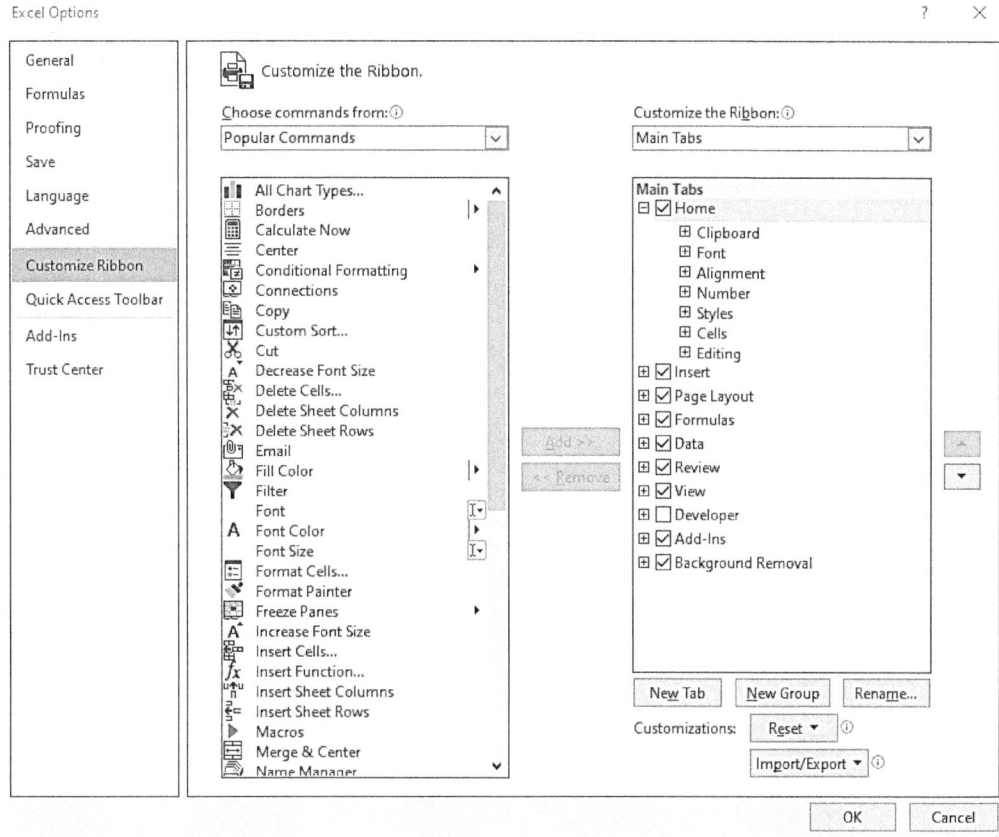

2.3 Worksheet in Excel

Other than Ribbon, the second thing that can be seen in excel is the worksheet. A worksheet is a single sheet with a group of cells under which the user can save, modify, and manipulate data. A worksheet can also be called a spreadsheet. Rows, Columns, and cells comprise up the structure.

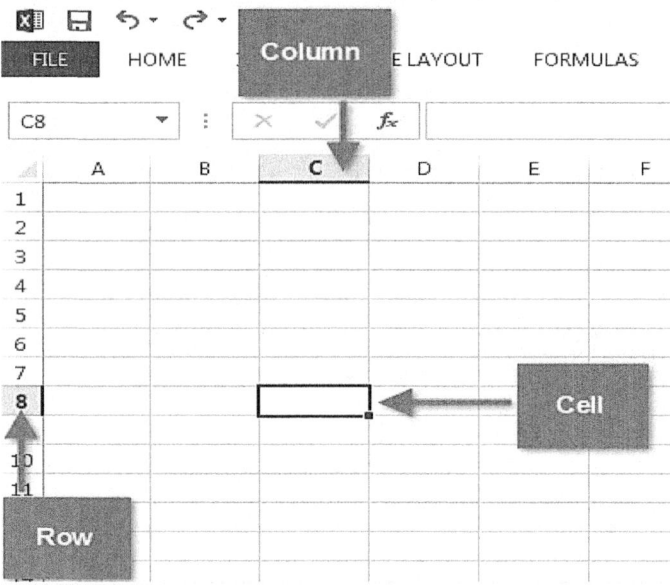

2.4 Row in Microsoft Excel

A row is a horizontal line in a spreadsheet. In a worksheet, there are 1048576 rows represented by numbers. A row can be inserted or deleted by clicking on the Insert Tab. Another option is to insert a row or delete a row is by right-clicking on the row and using the options of insert or delete.

'2.5 Column in Microsoft Excel

A column is a vertical line in a spreadsheet. In a worksheet, there are 16,384 columns represented by alphabets. The header can identify them. A column can be inserted or deleted by right-clicking on the column, and a dialogue box will pop up with options of deleting or inserting a column. Choose the option, "Entire Column."

Cell

A Cell can be defined as the intersection of a Row and a Column in an Excel spreadsheet in form of a rectangle. One cell can only store one piece of information at a time. Text, number, formula, date, and other types of data are all acceptable.

A Cell can be identified by a Cell Address, which comprises the Column letter and the Row number.

Cell Range

In an Excel file, a cell range is a collection of selected cells. This range usually is symmetrical (square), but it can also be made up of individual cells. A cell range is also be referenced in a formula. A spreadsheet defines a cell range by referencing the range's upper left cell (minimum value) and the range's lower suitable cell (highest value). Asymmetrical cell range can look like this. (A1:C6) denotes the range from the upper left cell A1 to the bottom suitable cell C6.

Cell Reference

A cell reference, also known as a cell address, is a formula that identifies a cell on a worksheet by combining a column letter with a row number. The cell at the intersection of column A and row 1 is designated as A1; the second cell in column B is designated as B2, and so on.

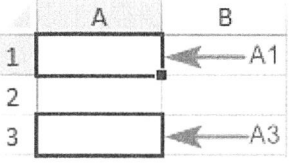

Range Reference

A range in Microsoft Excel is a group of two or more cells. A range reference is formed by separating the addresses of the upper left and bottom-right cells with a colon. The range A1:C2, for example, contains 6 cells numbered A1 through C2.

The notation (=A1:C6) denotes the range of cells A1 through C6. It has no meaning on its own, and Excel will produce the standard error #VALUE!

	A	B	C	D	E	F	G	H
1	2	56	8					
2	7	3	5					
3	56	7	8					
4	5	4	7					
5	3	3	4					
6	1	21	9		#VALUE!			
7								

Formula bar showing E6 =A1:C6

Formula Bar

The formula bar has three buttons or commands: Enter, Cancel, and Insert function. It is a thin bar located under the Ribbon of Excel and above the worksheet with a function symbol marked as *fx*. It has three components:

- Name box
- Formula bar buttons
- Cell contents box

The formula bar allows you to create new formulas or replicate current ones. When you type an equal sign in any cell or click anywhere within the formula bar, the formula bar is activated. It can be expanded according to your choice, vertically or horizontally, by a double-ended curser when you place your cursor around it. Hide it by clicking on the View Tab and checking on the Formula Bar option. Uncheck it to make it visible again.

You can use the formula bar to insert data into a cell by selecting the cell and clicking the input box in the formula bar. After you've finished entering the value, click the enter button on the left side of the formula bar. There's also a cancel data entering option, or you may use the escape key. There is an insert function icon (*fx*) on the formula bar, which, when clicked, opens a dialogue box in which you can find and enter the function.

- Select cell, click to insert function.
- Choose the function you want to add, click OK to bring up a dialogue box to define the function's arguments.
- In Excel's help menu, click Help on this function to understand more about it and view examples.
- Select the OK option.

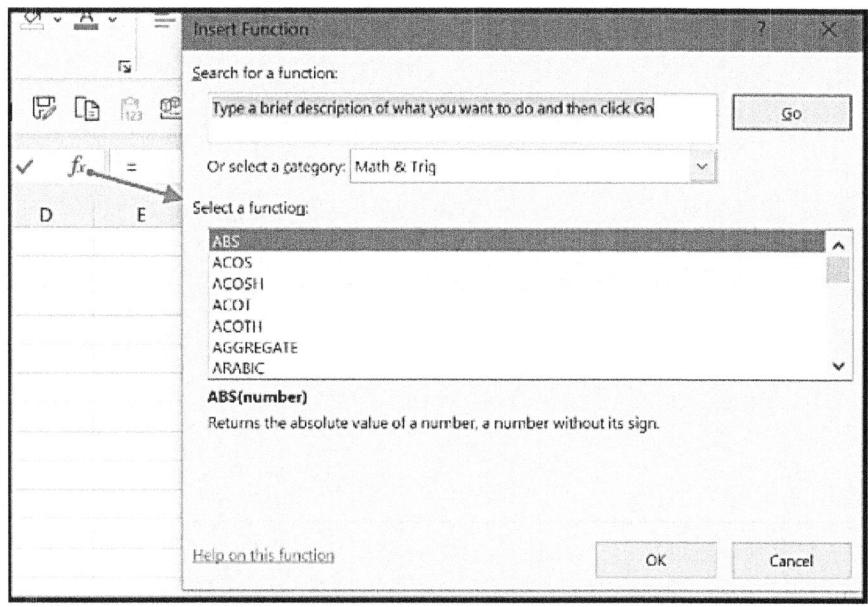

2.6 Other Commands on Excel Interface

The Quick Access toolbar is above the tabs row on Excel Ribbon. Add or remove commands from there. By default, it has three commands, File, Undo, and Repeat. Next to them, click on the drop-down menu and select more commands of your choice. For example, add a new document by selecting **New**.

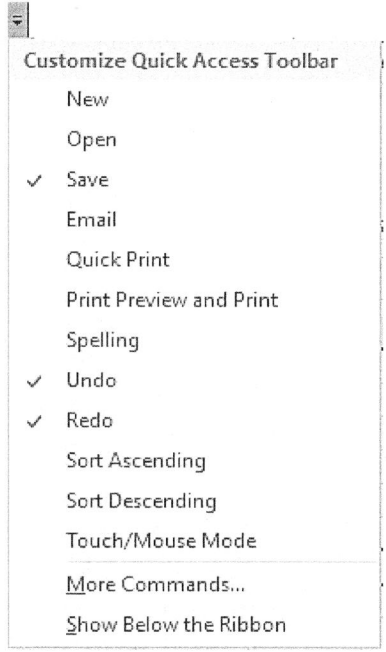

Name Box

The name box provides the active cell's address. Entering the address of another cell in the Name Box and clicking the Enter button will lead you to that cell.

Active Cell

Active cell shows the cell that is presently being highlighted. It is the cell where you last moved your mouse or pressed. On display, this cell is highlighted.

File Button

When you click the File Button, a drop-down menu appears with options such as open, save, and print.

Horizontal Scroll Bar

A horizontal Scroll Bar is used to scroll contents horizontally.

Vertical Scroll Bar

Vertical Scroll Bar is used to scroll contents vertically.

Zoom Bar

Zooming in and out of an Excel worksheet is done using the Zoom Bar. The zoom percentage is also displayed.

Windows Control

Window controls manage the default Excel window. Three buttons are used to minimize the window, maximize the window, restore the window and close the window, just like any other Windows application.

Status Bar

Status Bar contains specific data, including the sum, count, and average of any colored area by default.

Worksheet Tab

You can minimize, maximize, restore or close the worksheet using the worksheet control buttons. Also, other workbooks at the lower end of the left corner can be seen. Other spreadsheets can also be opened up that already exist on your computer. One workbook can contain many worksheets. See them at the lower end of your window, numbered as sheet1, sheet2 and sheet3 by default. After opening a workbook, a spreadsheet will be in front.

DAY #2

"Anyone who stops learning is old, whether at twenty or eighty. Anyone who keeps learning stays young."

Henry Ford

Chapter 3: Entering, Editing and Managing Data

This chapter discusses cell, entering data, modify, and delete, auto-fill about rows and columns. This section's learnings are often required in the early stages of creating worksheets.

3.1 Concept of Cell

As mentioned above, the intersection of a Row and a Column in an Excel spreadsheet is a rectangle called a Cell. Each cell was positioned on a worksheet, identified by the number row and column. For example, in the following picture, the highlighted cell is positioned as A1. Name box shows its position:

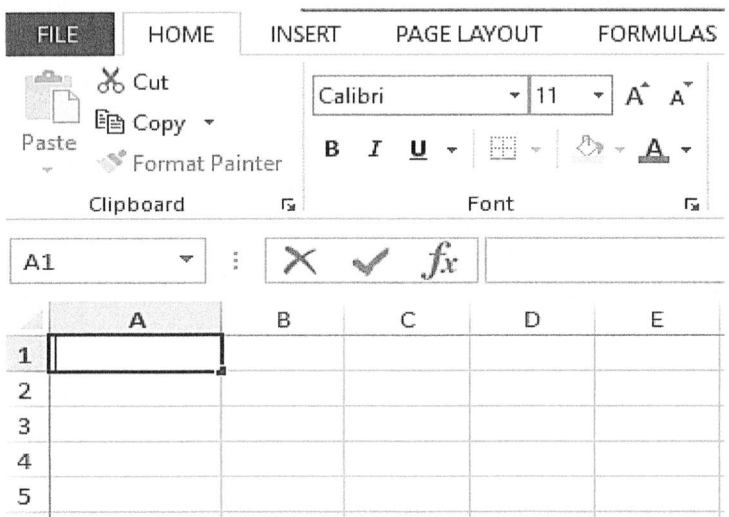

3.2 Enter Data in a Cell

To enter data in a cell, click on a cell or use arrow keys on the keyboard. A border will surround the selected cell, and the column and row sidebars will be highlighted. Until another cell is being picked in the worksheet, the cell will remain selected. Enter your data in the form of text, symbols, dates or numbers. Press Enter on your keyboard after inserting data into the selected cell. It will display the contents of the cell and formula bar. In the formula bar, you may also enter and edit cell content.

You might want to select a wider group of cells, or a cell range, at times. Click it and hold, then drag the mouse to highlight all of the adjacent cells you want to pick. To select the cell range you want, release the mouse button. Until you click the other cell in the worksheet, the cells will remain selected.

Example:

1. In the Sheet1 worksheet, click cell A15.
2. Press the ENTER key after typing the abbreviation Tot.
3. Select cell A15.
4. Up to the Formula Bar, move the mouse pointer. The pointer will change into a cursor. Left-click on the abbreviation Tot after moving the pointer to the end of it.
5. To finish the word Total, type the letters al.
6. To the opposite of the Formula Bar, click the checkbox. The change will be entered into the cell as a result of this.
7. Cell A15 should be double-clicked. Then After the phrase Total, type the word Purchase, followed by a space. Click the ENTER again.

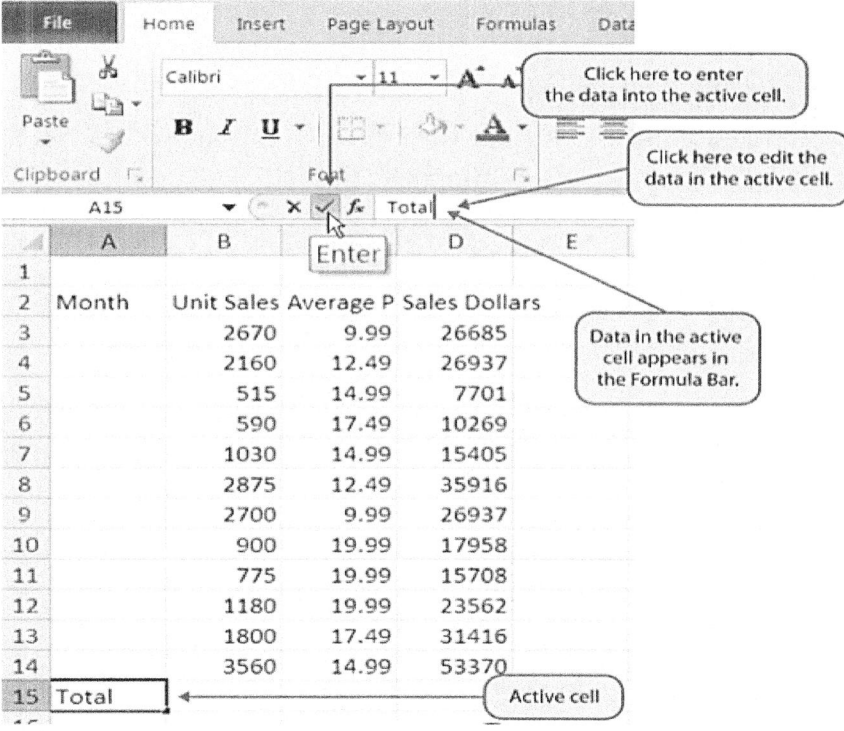

Move Data

You can move data in a worksheet to other areas once it has been added. The methods below show how to move data from one area on a worksheet to another:

1. You may highlight the range by activating your preferred cell and dragging it down

to the opposite cell.

2. Place the mouse pointer on the cell's left edge.
3. The white block + sign will transform into cross arrows. It means you can left-click the data and drag it to a new location.

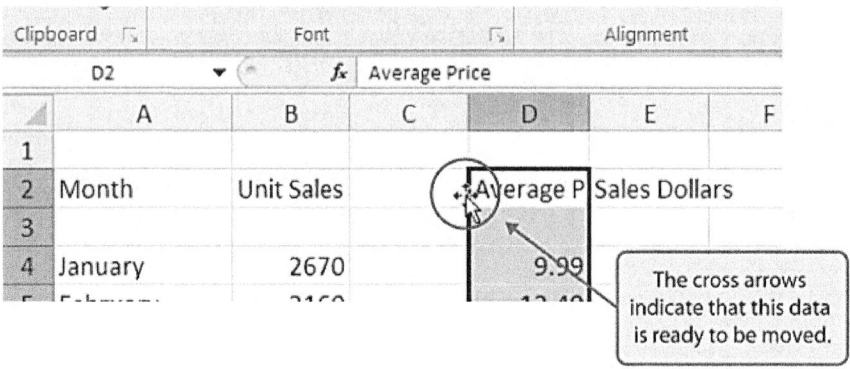

3.3 Modifying Data in Excel

- Double-click on the cell that contains the data you wish to modify.
- It will switch to edit mode and place the cursor in the cell where you double-clicked. The formula bar also shows the contents of the cells.
- Click anywhere in the formula bar after clicking the cell that contains the data you want to modify.
- It will switch to edit mode and place the cursor in the formula bar where you clicked.

Delete Data:

Select a cell range or a cell to delete the data, then click the backspace or delete button on the keyboard.

You can delete data from numerous cells at once by pressing the Delete key on your keyboard. Only one cell can be erased at a time with the Backspace key.

There are various methods for eliminating data from a spreadsheet. Undo command is also useful with each technique if data is accidentally deleted from your worksheet.

The instructions below show you how to erase data from a cell or a range of cells:

- Place your cursor over cell B2, and by clicking the left mouse button, you can select it.
- On your keyboard, press the DELETE key. The contents of the cell are removed as a result of this action.
- Place the mouse cursor over a cell to highlight the range. Then, with the mouse pointer on the left, drag down to cell C14.
- Place your cursor over the Fill Handle. The white block + symbol will be replaced by a black plus sign.
- Move the pointer up to cell C3 and release it. Release mouse clicks to be released. It will erase the range's contents.

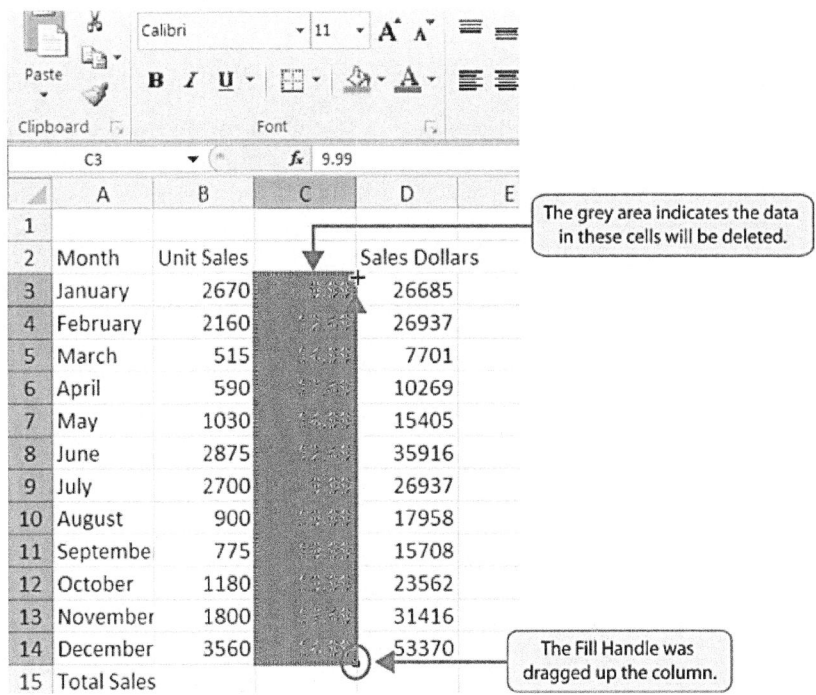

29

Auto-fill Data:

When manually inputting data into a worksheet, the AutoFill option comes in handy. This function is useful for a variety of tasks, but it is especially useful when typing data in a specific order, such as the numbers 1, 3, 5, 7, and so on, or qualitative data, such as the days of the week or months of the year.

1. Select a cell to enter your data; for example, you enter January in A3.
2. Press Enter.
3. Activate A3 cell again.
4. Place the pointer in cell A1's lower right corner. In this area of the cell, you'll notice a little square called the Fill Handle. The white block "+" sign will change into a dark plus sign as the cursor approaches the Fill Handle.
5. All twelve months of the year will appear in the cell range once you release the left mouse button. 'The AutoFill Options' will also be visible.

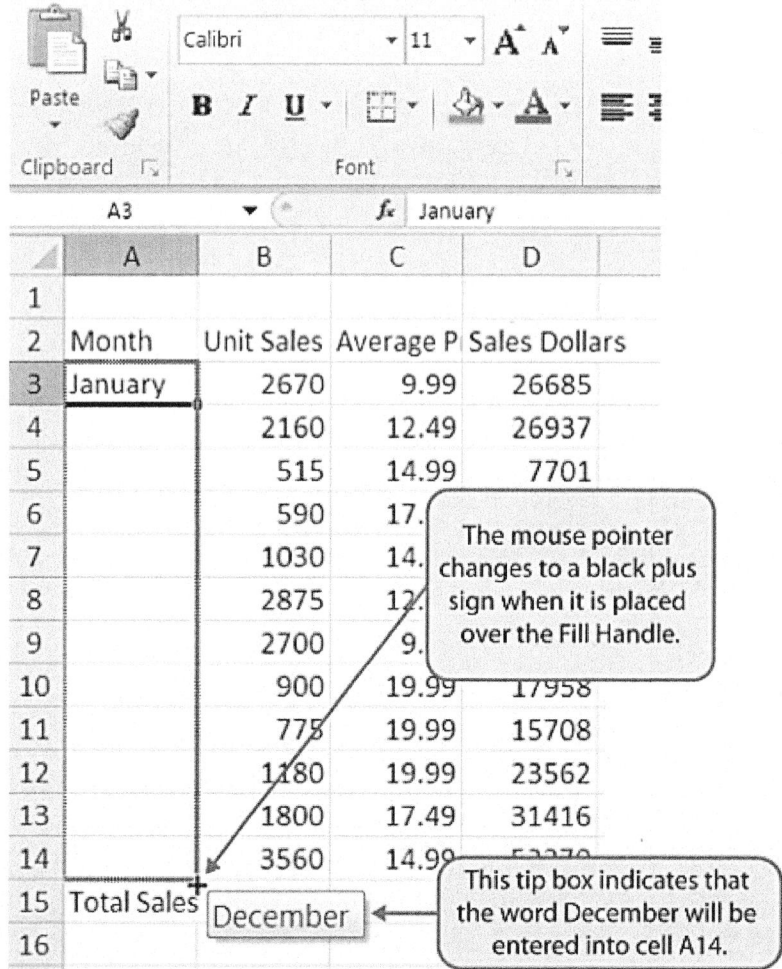

30

You have various options for putting data into a set of cells when you select this option:

- Select Auto Fill Options from the drop-down menu.
- Select Copy Cells from the drop-down menu. The months in the range will be changed to January as a result of this.
- Re-press the AutoFill button to open.
- To return the months of the year to the cell range, select Fill Months. The Fill Series option achieves the same outcome.

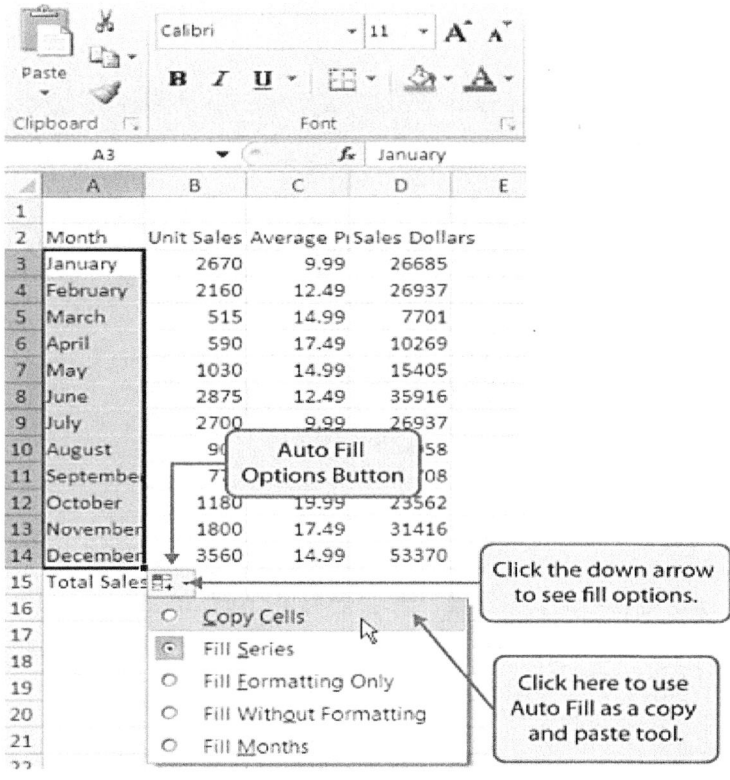

3.4 Rows and Columns

Insert new columns or rows, delete some rows or columns, move them to a different spot in the worksheet, or even conceal them after working with a workbook for a long.

Adjust the columns and rows in an Excel worksheet to fit the data entered into a cell. The methods below show how to change the column widths and row heights in a worksheet:

> In the Sheet1 spreadsheet, move the mouse pointer between Column A and Column B. The white block + sign will transform into double arrows.

➢ To see the complete word October or September in cell A11 or in cell A12, click and drag the column to the right. The column width box will appear as you drag the column. The number of characters that will fit into the column using the Calibri 11-point font, which is the default font/size configuration, is displayed in this box. Allow the left mouse button to be released. Just like the height of that row can be changed.

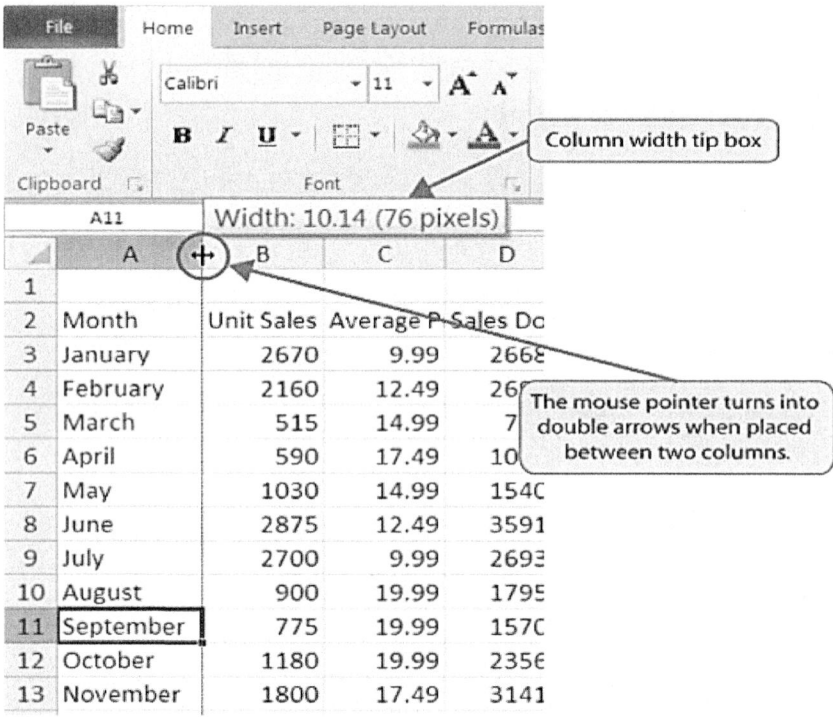

Another method to change the width of a column or height of a row is to right-click on the row or the column you want to change. A drop-down menu will appear. Click on the Row Height or Column Width Option and adjust them as you wish.

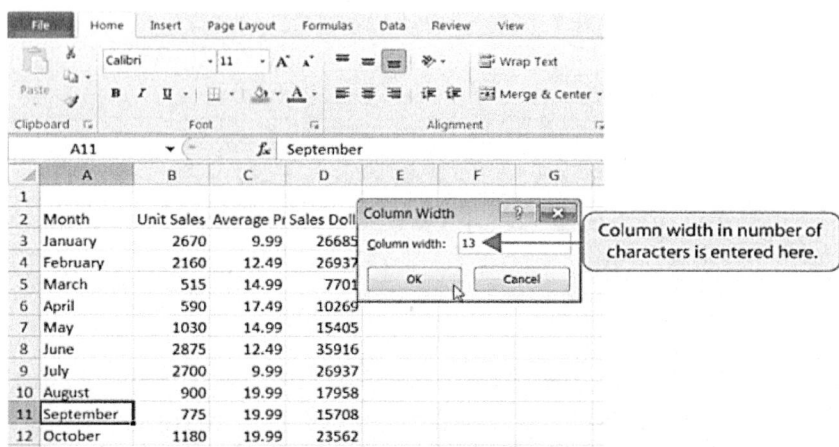

32

3.5 Hide or Unhide Row or Column

You can hide columns and rows on a worksheet in addition to changing them. It is a great strategy for improving the aesthetic appeal with data that are not required to be displayed:

- Click on any row or column.
- Right-click on that row or column, a drop-down menu will appear.
- Select the option of "Hide."
- The missing letter or number indicates that a column or a row is hidden.

Use the same method to unhide a row or a column. Highlight the range cells in a column or a row by dragging your mouse, selecting the area, and then right-click. A drop-down menu will appear select option unhide.

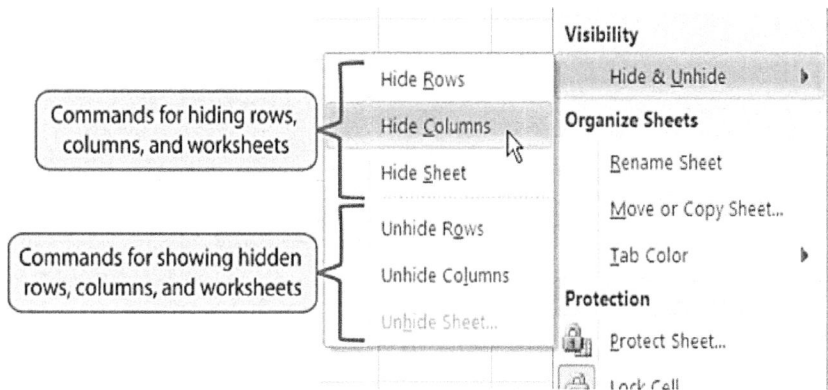

3.6 Insert or Delete Row or Column

Using pre-made Excel workbooks is a time-saving method of working because it avoids constructing data worksheets from scratch.

However, you may discover that you need to add or delete columns or rows of data to achieve your objectives.

In this situation, you can create a worksheet with blank columns or rows. The steps below will show you how to do it:

To insert a Column

1. Click on the cell in the column next to which you wish to insert a column.
2. After selecting the cell, left-click on it.

3. A drop-down menu will appear.
4. Select the option Insert.

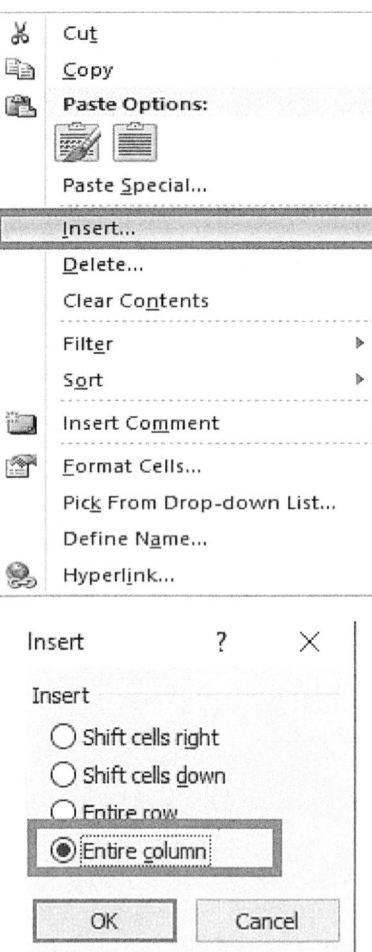

5. Click on the option **Insert entire Column.** Press **OK.** Or, in the "Home Tab", click on the Insert down arrow.
6. Select the option of **Insert Sheet Columns**.
7. A blank column next to the selected cell will appear.
8. Remember columns always are inserted left to activated cell.

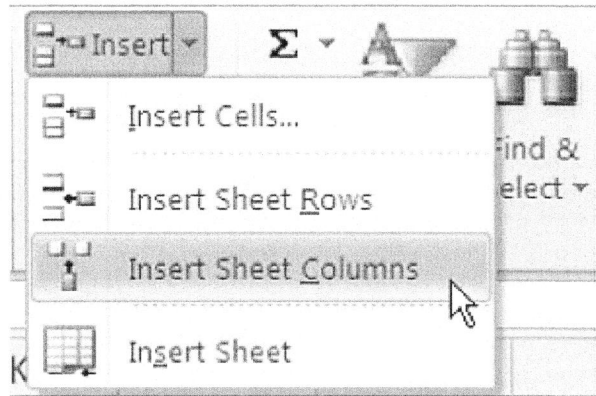

To insert a row:

1. Click on a cell in a row next to which you want to insert a row.
2. After selecting the cell, left-click on it.
3. A drop-down menu will appear.
4. Select the option Insert.
5. Click on the option **Insert entire Row.** Press **OK.**

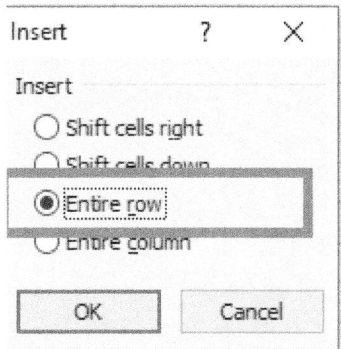

6. Or, in the "Home Tab", click on the Insert down arrow.
7. Select the option of **Insert Sheet Rows**.
8. A blank row below the selected cell will appear.
9. Remember, rows are always inserted above the activated cell.

To delete a Column:

1. You can select the appropriate cell by hovering the mouse pointer over the cell and clicking the left mouse button.
2. Select the **Delete** option, and then option.
3. **Entire Column**. Click the **OK** button.

4. Alternatively, in the "Home tab" of the Ribbon, click the down arrow on the Delete button in the Cells group.

5. From the drop-down menu, select the **Delete Sheet Columns** option. The column is removed, and all of the data in the worksheet is shifted next to one column.

<u>To delete a row:</u>

1. You can select the appropriate cell by hovering the mouse pointer over the cell and clicking the left mouse button.

2. Select the Delete option, and then option Delete the Entire Row. Click the **OK** button.

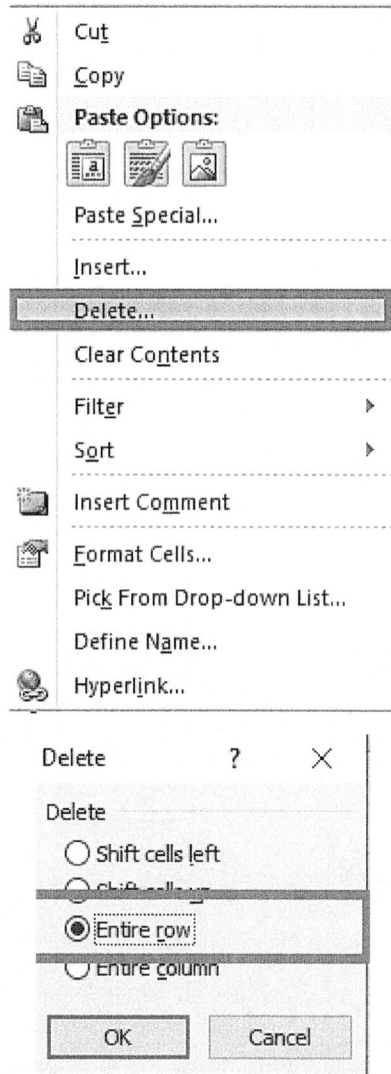

3. Alternatively, in the "Home tab" of the Ribbon, click the down arrow on the Delete

button in the Cells group.

4. From the drop-down menu, select the Delete Sheet Rows option. A row is removed, and all of the data in the worksheet is shifted up one row.

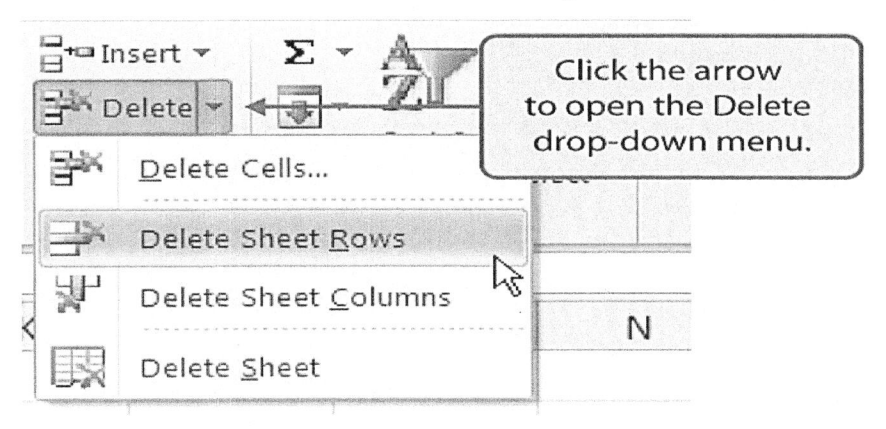

3.7 Moving Column or Row

You might want to alter the information of your worksheet by moving a column or row:

1. Please select a column to move from its heading, as A, B, C or D.
2. Click on the option of **Cut** on the Home menu.
3. Then choose the column heading to the right of the column you wish to move. Select column G, for example, if you wish to relocate a column between F and H columns.
4. Select Insert Cut Cells from the drop-down menu after clicking the Insert command on the "Home tab."
5. It will move the column to the desired location.
6. Or right-click on the selected cells or data from a row or a column.
7. Then select the option of Cut from the drop-down menu and paste them where you want.

	A	B	C	D	E
1	ID Number	Hours Active	Errors	Efficiency	
2	Computer 1	281	5	42	
3	Computer 2	112	2	44	
4	Computer 3	126	7	42	
5	Computer 4	300	12	38	
6					
7	Computer 5	233	12	38	
8	Computer 6	362	6	37	
9	Computer 7	306	10	48	
10	Computer 8	200	38	50	
11	Computer 9	123	22	22	
12	Computer 10	213	7	33	
13	Computer 11	344	2	21	
14	Computer 12	221	4	42	
15	Computer 13	182	2	46	
16	Computer 14	308	7	41	
17	Computer 15	360	10	21	
18	Computer 16	273	5	12	
19	Computer 17	277	11	33	
20	Computer 18	221	9	32	
21	Computer 19	222	6	50	
22	Computer 20	297	8	18	

3.8 To Swap Rows and Columns

Copy and paste are not the only option rows and columns can also be swapped. You don't have to build a new row; swapping data across nearby rows is significantly easier. Holding Shift on your keyboard allows you to quickly switch data between two columns or rows in Excel. Here's what you should do:

1. Select the data of the row or column you want to swap.

2. On your keyboard, press and hold the "Shift" key.

3. Hover your cursor over the border between two adjacent rows until a cross-arrow icon appears.

4. Click and hold "Shift" on your mouse until a grey line appears beneath the row you want to switch the data with.

Release the mouse click, and the data will swap locations. You can swap between columns using the same approach.

	A	B	C	D
1	ID Number	Hours Active	Errors	Efficiency
2	Computer 1	281	5	42
3	Computer 2	112	2	44
4	Computer 3	126	7	42
5	Computer 4	300	12	38
6	Computer 5	306	10	48
7	Computer 6	362	6	37
8	Computer 7	233	13	38
9	Computer 8	200	38	50
10	Computer 9	123	22	22
11	Computer 10	213	7	33
12	Computer 11	344	2	21
13	Computer 12	271	4	42
14	Computer 13	182	2	46
15	Computer 14	308	7	41
16	Computer 15	360	10	21
17	Computer 16	273	5	12
18	Computer 17	277	11	33
19	Computer 18	221	9	32
20	Computer 19	222	6	50
21	Computer 20	297	8	18

Chapter 4: Working with Worksheets

4.1 What is a worksheet?

A spreadsheet is a file in Microsoft excel which is used to organize, compute, and sort data. Numeric numbers, text, formulae, references, and functions can all be added to a spreadsheet. The rows and columns in the Worksheet are used to organize the cells. From 1 at the top through 1,048,576 at the bottom, each row is labeled with a number.

The letters A through XFD are used to designate the columns in order from left to right. As there are only 26 alphabets, the column labeling method begins with A to Z assigned to the first 26 columns, then proceeds on to AA, AB,..., AZ, BA, BB,... until we reach ZZ, at which point the procedure repeats itself at AAA and continues until the 16,384th column is labeled XFD. A cell is formed by combining a column and a row, and its address can be fixed by the column letter and row number.

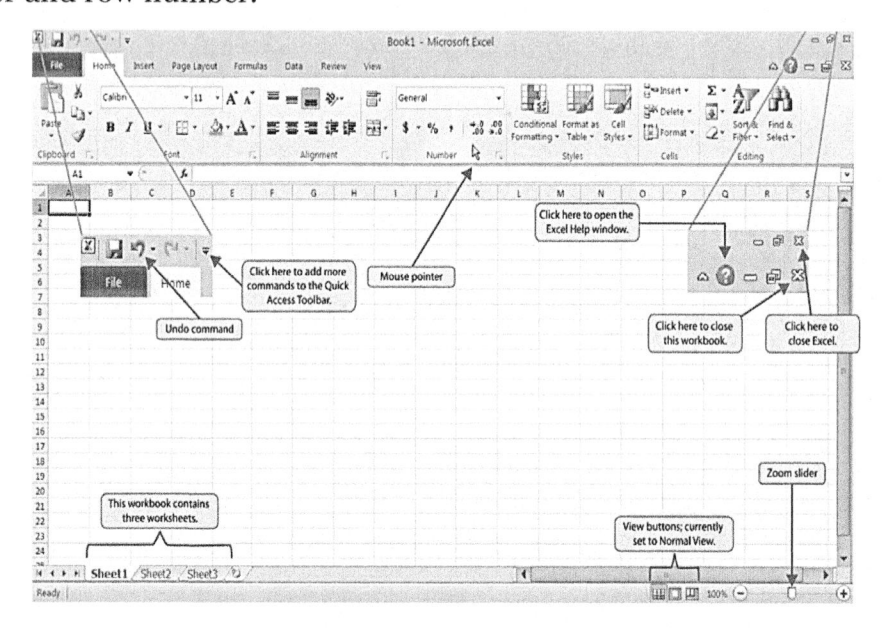

4.2 Cell in Worksheet

The active cell is inside the Worksheet, where any fresh data or formula may be added or modified. The active cell in a spreadsheet may be detected using the techniques below:

- A broad dark green border encloses the cell.
- The dark grey color is used for the corresponding column and row.

- In the Name box, the cell's location is mentioned.

4.3 Difference between Workbook and Worksheet

The fundamental difference between a worksheet and a workbook is that a worksheet is a single-page spreadsheet or page in Excel where you may write, modify, and change data, whereas a workbook is a collection of similar worksheets. The following are some further distinctions between a workbook and a worksheet:

- It's considerably easier to link two worksheets than it is to link two workbooks. Many times, linking workbooks causes data security concerns.
- Worksheets, not workbooks, are the sole way to manipulate and analyze data. The workbook is only the front page or face of the data.
- It is simple to add numerous worksheets to a workbook. However, it is more difficult to add a workbook to another workbook.
- A worksheet is a section of a workbook.

4.4 Excel Worksheet Tab

At the bottom of the Worksheet, you'll see the worksheet tabs. You can go straight to that page of your workbook by clicking on the tab. More worksheets can be added, deleted, the worksheet title changed, and color fill added to the tab. At the left bottom of the workbook, you'll find the worksheet tabs.

Excel comes with three worksheets titled Sheet 1, Sheet 2, and Sheet 3 by default. The active Worksheet is only visible at one time. The workbook can have any number of sheets added or deleted. Different commands can use to do the formatting of a spreadsheet.

4.5 How to add a new Worksheet?

At any position in the sheet tab list, more sheets can be added at any time. The number and position of added sheets are determined by the number and position of the workbook's selected sheets. The easiest way to add the spreadsheet is to Click the + mark at the right end of the worksheet window to rapidly insert a new worksheet. Other than that, there are two methods to add a worksheet:

- By Using Ribbon Command.

- Right-Click Method.

In **the Ribbon Command method,** click the home menu in the ribbon. Begin by selecting the Home menu from the ribbon. Then search in the Cells command grouping. Then click insert. Select the Insert Sheet option.

While in **Right-Click Method,** do right-click in the worksheet tab, select insert from the menu, and click OK. The new sheet will insert.

4.6 How to delete the Worksheet?

Sheet names are displayed in separate tabs at the bottom of the spreadsheet. You can delete any worksheet by following any of the procedures written below:

- Right-click method.
- Using Format option.

In **Right-click method**, do a right-click on the spreadsheet tab, press the delete option from the drop-down list, and click OK. The sheet is going to be deleted.

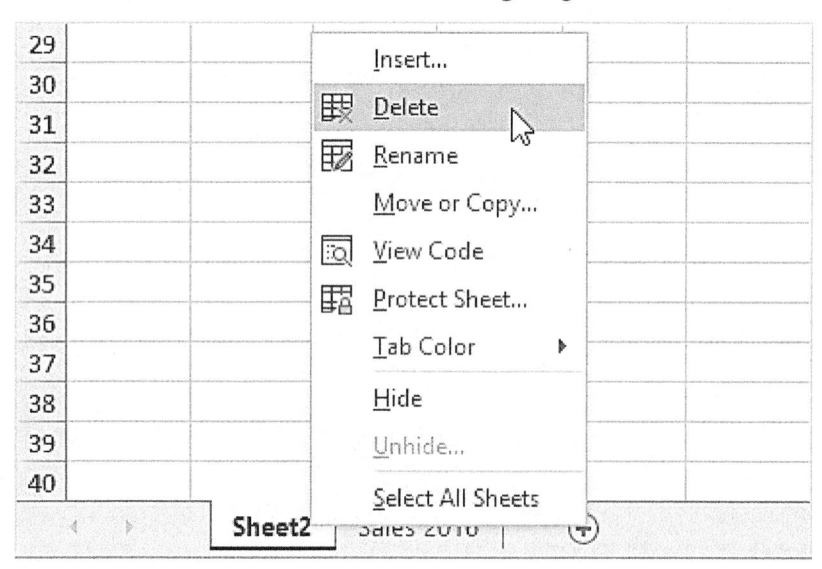

Using **Format Option**, delete a spreadsheet. Click the Worksheet to delete at the bottom of the workbook. Choose Delete under the new label "Cells" and click Delete Sheet on the Home tab afterward.

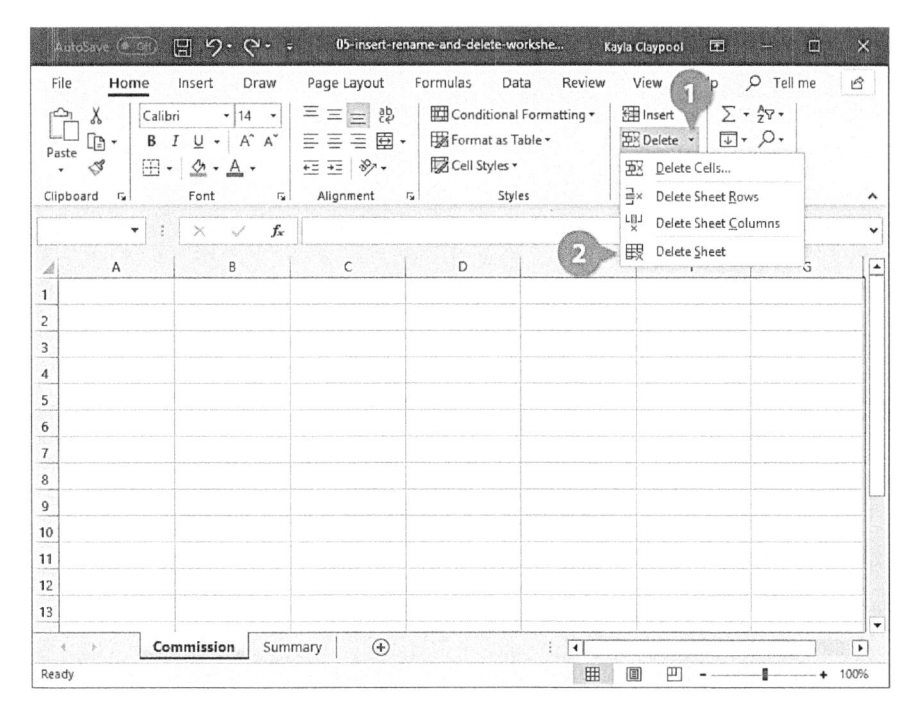

There is no way to redo the deletion and regain data once the spreadsheet has been erased from the workbook.

4.7 How to Copy Worksheet

There are three ways to replicate spreadsheets in Excel:
- Using Drag method
- Using Right-click method.
- Using Format method.

Dragging a sheet to another area within the workbook is the simplest and most basic way to replicate it. To make a duplicate sheet, choose the Worksheet. Hold down the control key.

To make a copy, drag and drop the selected sheet.

Right-clicking on any worksheet tab and selecting Move or Copy from the menu that appears to replicate worksheets. Toggle the Create a copy box on, then click OK.

In the Name box, the cell's location has mentioned.

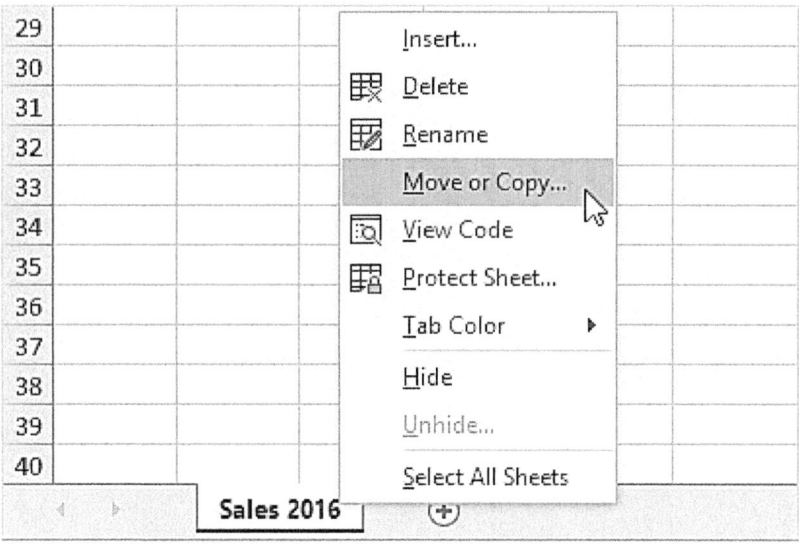

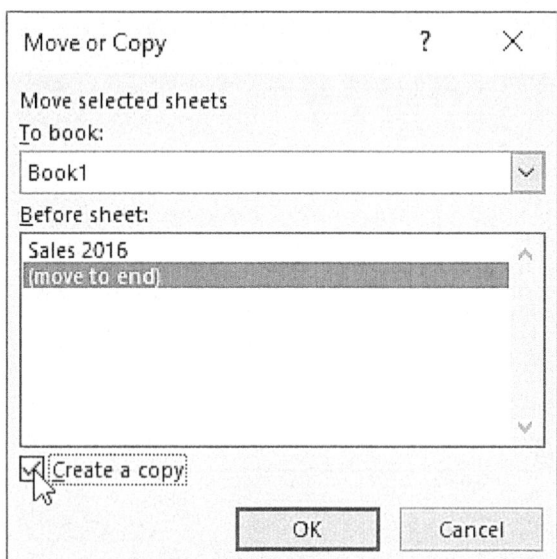

In Excel, you can replicate a worksheet using the **Format section** of the ribbon.

To duplicate a worksheet, first open it. Click Cells group on the Home tab, select Format, then Move or Copy Sheet. Choose a place for the copy to be saved. Make a copy by checking the Create a Copy box. Click the OK button.

Worksheets in Microsoft Excel can be copied to some other workbook:

- To move or copy a sheet, use the right-click menu. From the menu, choose Move or Copy.
- To move or copy a sheet to other workbooks, choose a new worksheet from the menu that appears. Choose where to copy the sheet.

- To make a copy of the sheet, tick the Create a copy box.
- To make a copy, press the OK button.

4.8 How to Change Color of Worksheet

In Microsoft Excel, a selected Spreadsheet Tab is white but it can be added a splash of color or distinguishing colors. Adding color to Worksheet Tabs is a simple method to organize work and distinguish them from one another.

The methods for changing the color of the worksheet tab are as follows:

1. Click on the Worksheet tab.
2. In the Cell Group section of the Home Tab, Select Format on the left to bring up a drop-down list.
3. Right-click the Spreadsheet Tab and select Tab Color. The color of the worksheet tab will change.

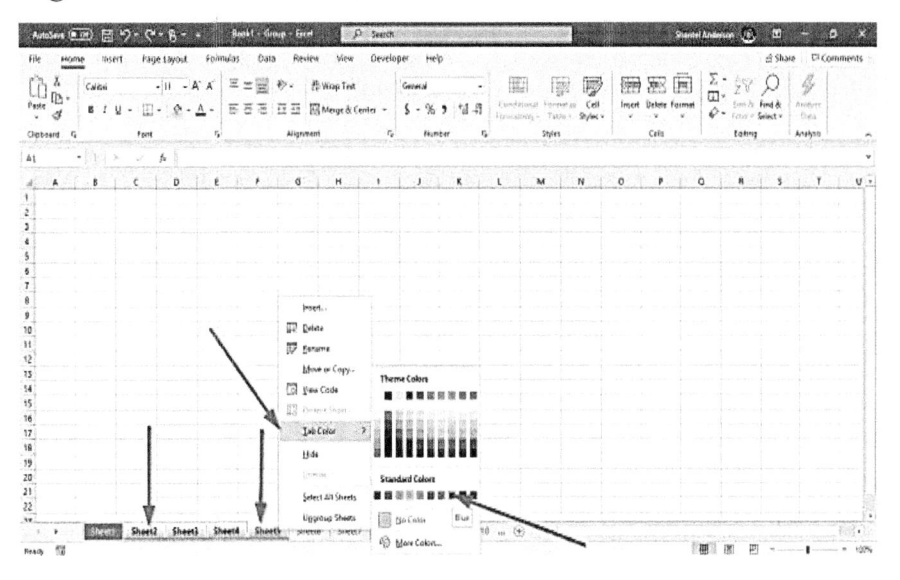

4.9 Grouping and Ungrouping of Worksheet

Sheets may be grouped to make it easier to create or prepare two similar sheets. For example, create one sheet and copy it to two additional sheets, or combine three blank pages and input and format the information all at once, eliminating the need for future copying. The **"GROUP AND UNGROUP"** feature makes it simple to handle rows and columns. All the rows are combined into a single structure that may be compressed or extended as needed. Both methods are easy to use and very helpful when dealing with huge amounts of information.

4.10 To Group Worksheet

To group the consecutive worksheets, click the sheet icon of the first sheet you want to include in the group. While pressing down the SHIFT key, press the final sheet in the group. Between the first and final selected sheets, all sheets are grouped.

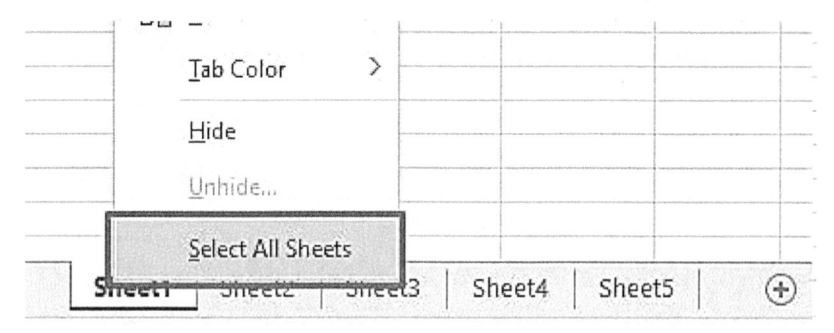

4.11 Benefits of Grouping Worksheets

Many of the things that can accomplish using grouped sheets are as follows:
- Fill in the same information in the same cells on all of the sheets.
- At the same time, update existing data on several spreadsheets.
- Apply the identical formulae to all of the sheets at the same time.
- Ensure that all of the sheets have the same formatting.

4.12 Ungrouping of Worksheets

Here are several methods for ungrouping sheets in Excel:
- The first approach is fairly straightforward. Choose any body from the tabs that aren't part of the group. The group edit option will be disabled as a result of this.

On the other hand, all of the sheets in a workbook are grouped; clicking on any single worksheet tab from the group will ungroup all of the sheets.
- The second method is to right-click from one of the group's worksheet tabs and choose "Ungroup Sheets" from the popup menu.

- To ungroup only one worksheet from a grouping, hold down the SHIFT key while clicking on the chosen sheet in the grouped tabs.

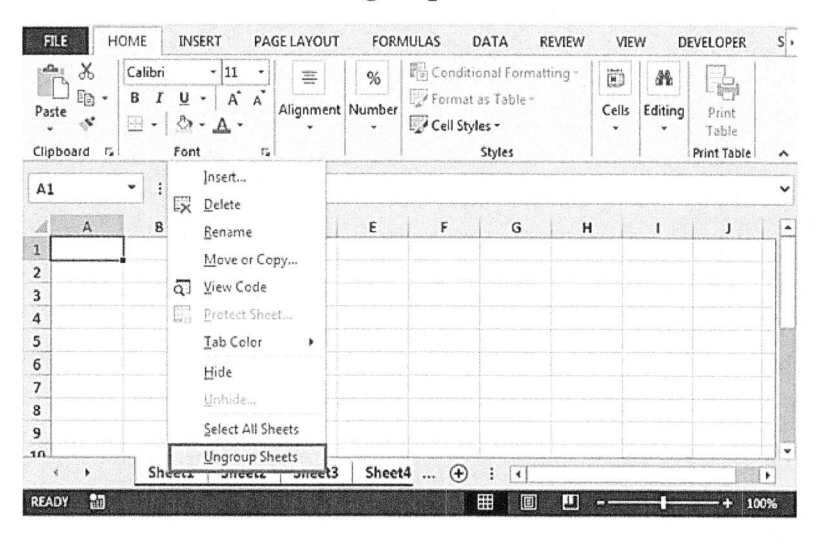

4.13 How to Identify Grouped Sheets

Determine whether or not the sheets in the workbook have been grouped before ungrouping them. There are two key features of grouped sheets:

- The sheets that are linked together typically have a white backdrop on their tabs. Those who do not belong to the group have a grey backdrop.
- In the Excel Title bar, the word 'Group' has been inserted as a prefix to the workbook's title.

4.14 Why Ungroup Worksheets?

Grouping sheets may help to save time and execute a set of actions consistently across many sheets. Once grouped, however, any modifications made to one page are duplicated across all sheets in the group. That may result in the unintended modification of data in certain spreadsheets. Furthermore, making modifications to particular sheets becomes challenging. In such situations, ungrouping the previously collected data may be beneficial.

DAY #3

"Those who never make mistakes lose a great many chances to learn something."

Mary Pickford

Chapter 5: Sorting and Filtering Data

Sorting data can help you quickly restructure a worksheet. A list of contact information, for example, could be organized by the last name. This chapter discusses sorting and filtering data alphabetically, numerically, and in various other ways possible.

5.1 Sorting data

Before sorting data, you must first decide whether to sort a cell range or the entire worksheet. One column organizes all the data on your worksheet. When the Sort is applied, related information from every row is kept together. The Contact Name column in the sample below has been sorted to display the names in alphabetical order. When working with a sheet with numerous tables, sorting a range sorts the data in a range of cells, which might be useful. Other texts on the worksheet will not be affected by sorting a range.

5.2 To sort data of a Sheet

1. We'll sort a T-shirt order form alphabetically by Last Name in the example given. (Column C).

	A	B	C	D	E
1	Homeroom #	First Name	Last Name	T-Shirt Size	Payment Method
2	105	Christiana	Chen	Medium	Check Bounced
3	105	Derek	MacDonald	Large	Cash
4	105	Esther	Yaron	Small	Pending
5	105	Melissa	White	Small	Debit Card
6	105	Nathan	Albee	Medium	Check
7	105	Sidney	Kelly	Medium	Check
8	110	Gabriel	Del Toro	Medium	Cash
9	110	Kris	Ackerman	Large	Money Order

2. Choose a cell in the column that you'd want to sort by. We'll use cell C2 as an example.

3. Click the A-Z command to sort A to Z or the Z-A command to sort Z to A on the Ribbon's Data tab. We'll sort A to Z, for example.

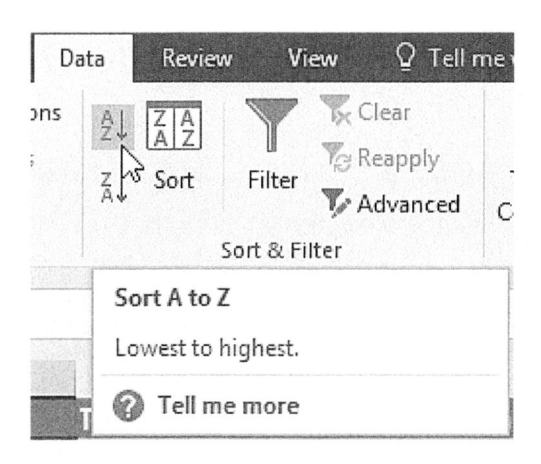

4. The selected column will be used to sort the worksheet. The last name will sort the worksheet in the example.

	A	B	C	D	E
1	Homeroom #	First Name	Last Name	T-Shirt Size	Payment Method
2	110	Kris	Ackerman	Large	Money Order
3	105	Nathan	Albee	Medium	Check
4	220-B	Samantha	Bell	Medium	Check
5	110	Matt	Benson	Medium	Money Order
6	105	Christiana	Chen	Medium	Check Bounced
7	110	Gabriel	Del Toro	Medium	Cash
8	220-A	Brigid	Ellison	Small	Cash
9	220-A	Juan	Flores	X-Large	Pending

5.3 To sort data of Cell Range

1. Choose the cell range that you'd want to sort.

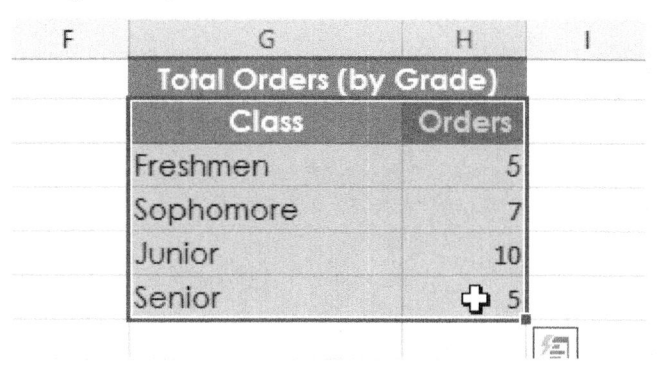

2. On the Ribbon, pick the Data tab, then the Sort command.

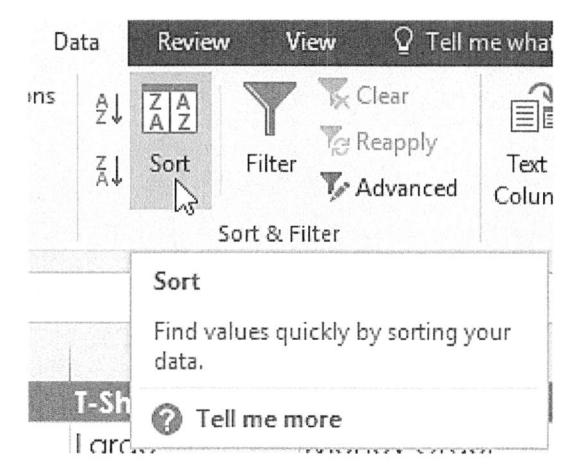

3. A dialogue box for sorting will display. Select the column that you'd want to sort by.

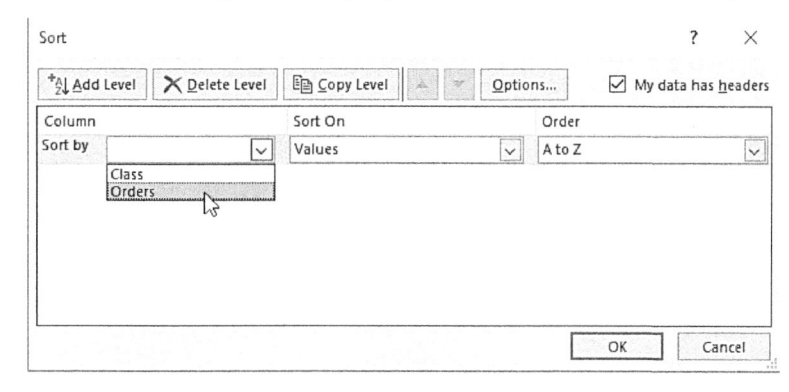

4. Choose ascending or descending order.

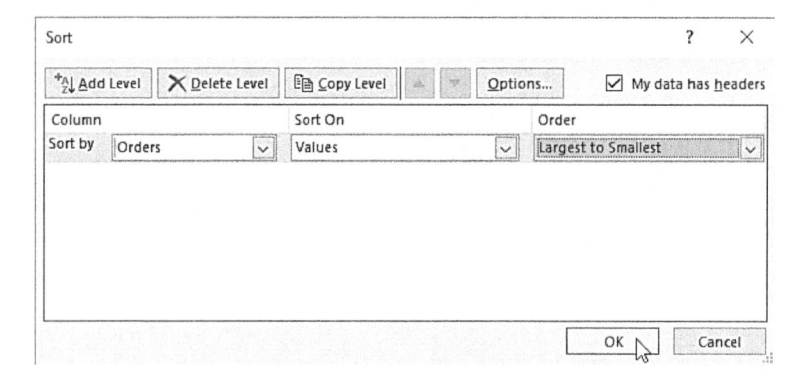

5. Click OK.

The selected column will be used to sort the cell range. The Orders column will be ordered from highest to lowest, for example. It's worth noting that the Sort did not affect the rest of the worksheet's information.

5.4 To Sort Data in one column

Execute the steps below to sort on a single column:

1. Select any cell in the column to sort by clicking on it.
2. Click AZ to sort in ascending order in the Sort & Filter group on the Data tab.

5.5 To Sort Data in multiple Columns

Execute the steps below to sort on multiple columns:

1. Select Sort from the Sort & Filter group on the Data tab.
2. The Sort dialogue box is displayed.
3. From the 'Sort by' dropdown menu, choose Last Name.
4. Select Add Level from the dropdown menu.
5. From the 'Then by' dropdown list, choose Sales.
6. Select OK.
7. Result. The records are arranged by Last Name first, then by Sales in the example.

5.6 Custom Sorting

The default sorting options may not always be able to sort data in the order you require. Fortunately, Excel allows you to establish your sorting order by creating a custom list.

A quick word on Custom Sort: This option allows you to choose how your data is sorted within a column. For example, rather than sorting information alphabetically, you might wish to arrange it by size. You'll need to make a custom list for your sort order in this scenario.

1. Select the data you want to sort by clicking on it.
2. Select Custom Sort from the dropdown menu after clicking the Sort command.

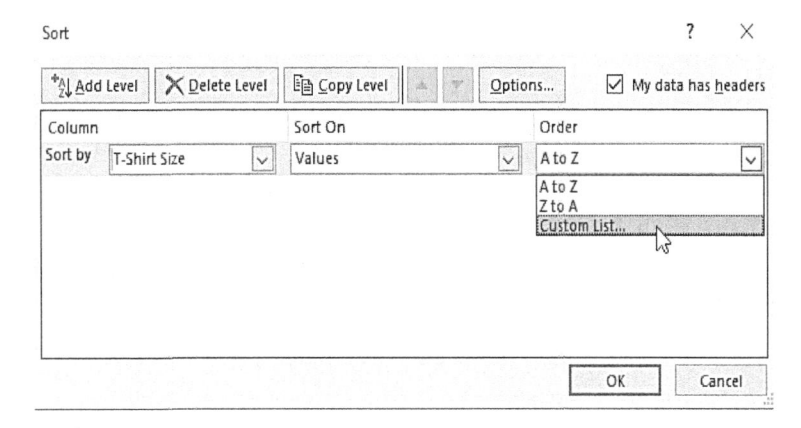

3. The Sort window will appear, allowing you to choose which column and how to sort it.
4. You can either use the default selections (weekdays or months) or create a new list. Select Custom List from the Order column, then NEW LIST to create a new list.

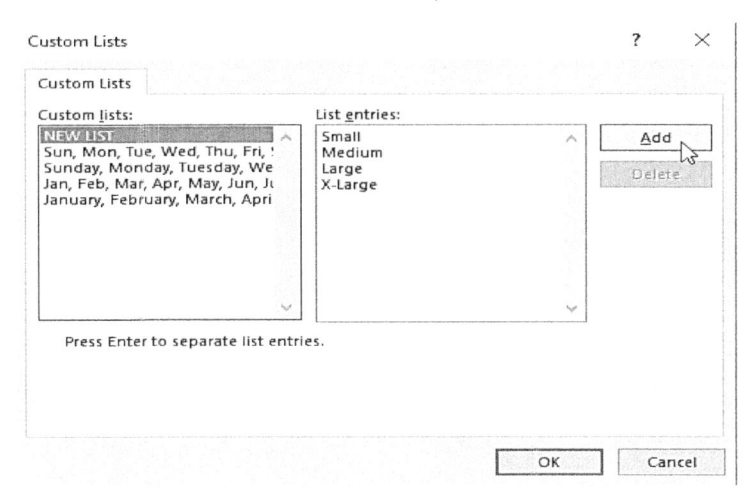

5. If you're constructing a custom list, type the order you want the data to be sorted. An example is sorting by size from tiny to large.

6. Your custom ordering list will show in the original Order dropdown menu after you click add.

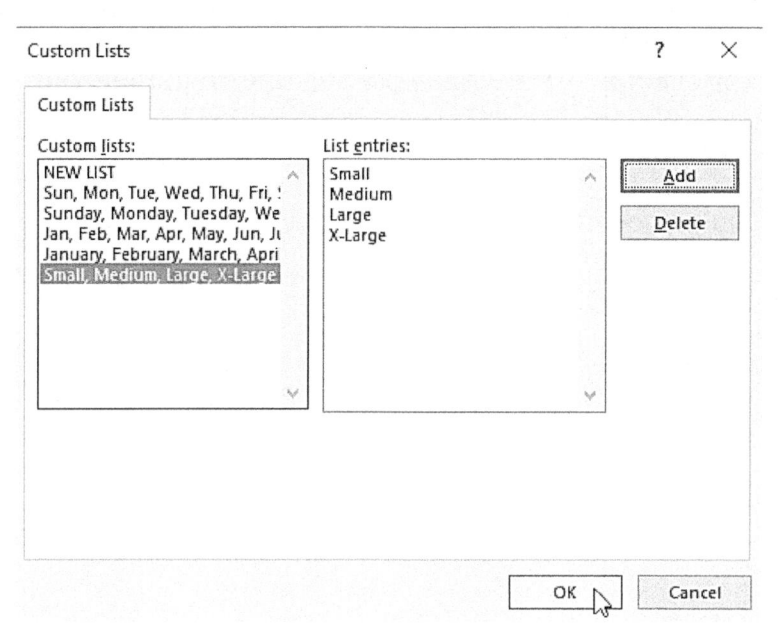

7. After that, select your personalized list and click OK.

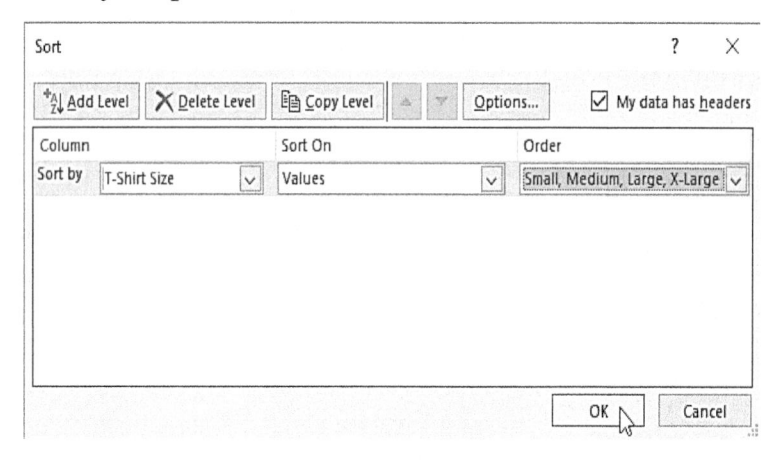

8. It will sort the data.

	A	B	C	D	E
1	Homeroom #	First Name	Last Name	T-Shirt Size	Payment Method
2	220-A	Brigid	Ellison	Small	Cash
3	220-B	Michael	Lazar	Small	Cash
4	135	Anisa	Naser	Small	Check Bounced
5	220-A	Christopher	Peyton-Gomez	Small	Check
6	220-B	Malik	Reynolds	Small	Cash
7	220-B	Wendy	Shaw	Small	Cash
8	105	Melissa	White	Small	Debit Card
9	105	Esther	Yaron	Small	Pending
10	105	Nathan	Albee	Medium	Check
11	220-B	Samantha	Bell	Medium	Check
12	110	Matt	Benson	Medium	Money Order
13	105	Christiana	Chen	Medium	Check Bounced
14	110	Gabriel	Del Toro	Medium	Cash
15	105	Sidney	Kelly	Medium	Check
16	220-B	Avery	Kelly	Medium	Debit Card
17	220-A	Chevonne	Means	Medium	Money Order
18	135	James	Panarello	Medium	Check
19	135	Chantal	Weller	Medium	Debit Card
20	110	Kris	Ackerman	Large	Money Order
21	105	Derek	MacDonald	Large	Cash

5.7 To Sort Data in a Row

Rather than sorting data by columns, you can sort it by row. We'll sort a monthly sales table in this example so that the month with the highest sales total is on the left. We'll use a right-click popup menu to accomplish this.

Follow these steps to sort by row:

1. Choose a cell in the row that you'd want to sort.
2. To select the entire region, press Ctrl + A.
3. Check that all of the data is included in the designated area.
4. To sort a row, right-click a cell in the row you wish to sort.
5. Click Sort, then Custom Sort in the popup menu.

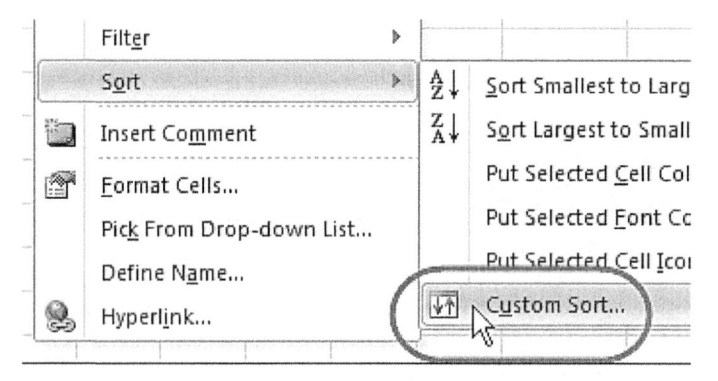

6. Select the column in 'Sort By box' in the Sort dialogue box.
7. Select Custom List from the Order dropdown menu.

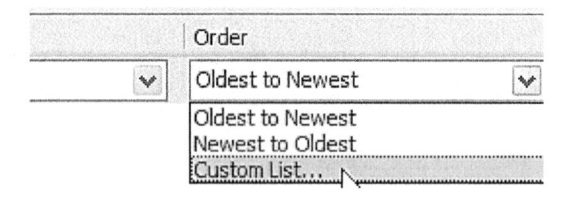

8. Click Options at the top of the Sort dialogue box.
9. Select Sort Left to Right from the Orientation dropdown menu in the Options dialogue box.
10. To close the Options dialogue box, click OK.
11. Select the row you want to sort from the Sort By dropdown menu. Because there are no headings, choose the correct Row number.

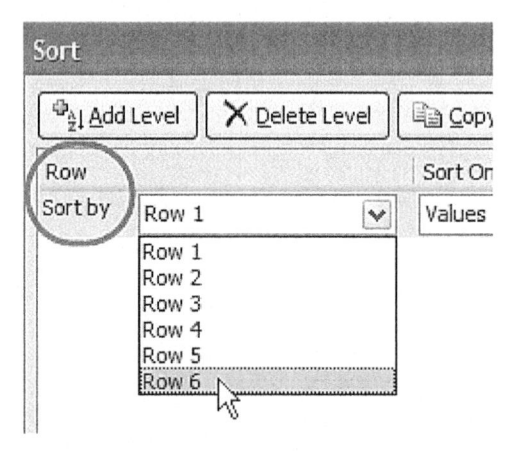

12. Click OK after selecting the Sort On and Order choices.
13. The values in the selected row are used to sort the data.

5.8 Sorting by Conditional formatting

The most commonly used feature in a spreadsheet is conditional formatting, which allows users to apply formats to a cell or group. A set of criteria usually determines the formats. It makes it easier to spot differences in cell values at a glance. For instance, you have two entries that are either true or false. For simple identification of circumstances, you might use a custom color scheme.

Implementing Conditional Formatting to more than one cell is the same as adding one or more formulas to each cell. As a result, applying Conditional Formatting to a large number of cells may degrade performance. When working with vast ranges, be cautious. Many datasets contain icons created using Excel's Conditional Formatting. You can sort the data in a specific order depending on these icons.

Icon sets replace regular conditional formatting choices that focus on font and cell formatting modifications.

To sort data:

1. Select a range of cells.
2. Select Sort & Filter option, then Custom Sort from the Home tab.
3. Choose the column holding the conditional icons from the Column dropdown arrow.
4. Select Conditional Formatting Icon from the Sort using the dropdown arrow.
5. Choose a color from the dropdown arrow under the order, for example, green.

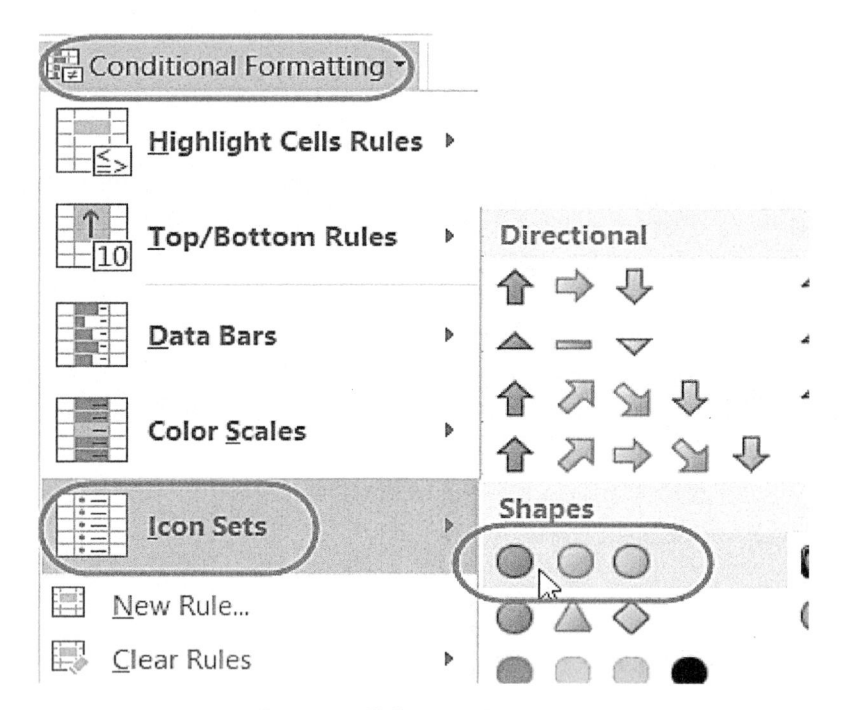

6. The color icon items you chose will be at the top of the list if you select on the top from the dropdown list next to the sort order box.

7. To add a second sort level, select Add.

8. Use the same parameters as the previous sort level, but select another color from the Order dropdown arrow. For example, choose yellow.

9. Select Create to add a third sort level, then apply the same parameters as the first two levels, but this time choose a different hue from the Order dropdown arrow, such as Red.

10. It will sort the data then close the dialogue box by selecting OK.

11. At the top of the data range, entries with the green icon are placed together, followed by entries with the yellow icon, and records with the red icon.

5.9 Filtering Data

The filter in Excel aids in the display of pertinent data by temporarily removing unnecessary elements from the screen. The information is filtered according to a specified criteria. The goal of sorting is to concentrate on the most important aspects of an information set. For example, an organization's city-level sales data can be filtered by location. Then, the user can see the sales of several cities at any one time.

Working with a large database necessitates the use of a filter. The filter, a widely used tool, transforms a complex view into one that is simple to comprehend. The dataset must have a header row that provides the name of each column to apply filters.

Working with filters is beneficial because they cater to our specific requirements. To filter data, check the boxes next to the entries you want to see and uncheck the boxes of the ones you don't.

The following are the three methods for adding filters to Excel:

- Under the Home tab, there is a filter option.
- Under the Data tab, there is a filter option.
- Using a shortcut key

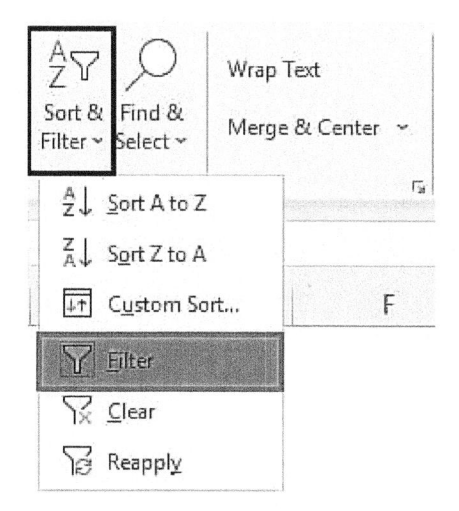

Method 1:

1. Under the "Sort and Filter" dropdown, select the data and click Filter in Home Tab.

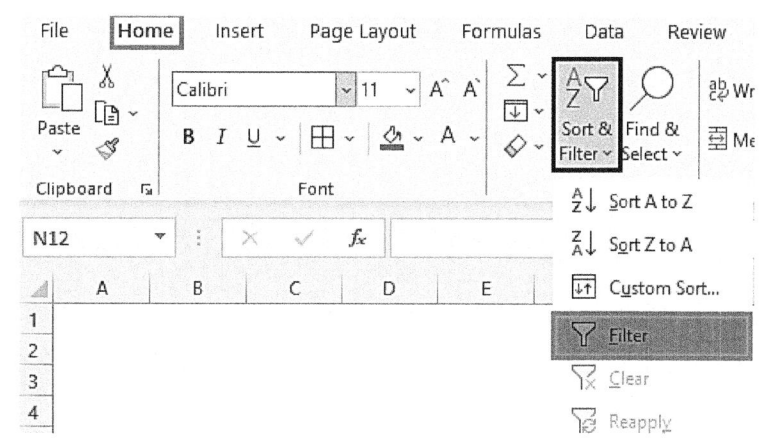

2. The filters are applied to the data range that has been chosen. Filters are the

dropdown arrows within the red boxes.

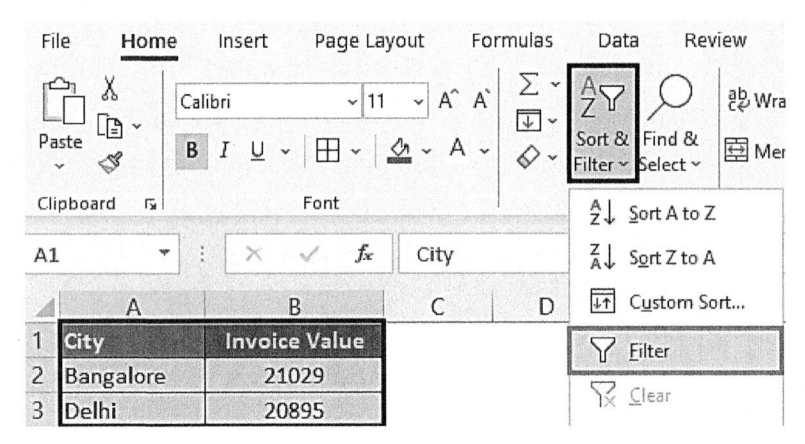

3. To see the different names of the cities, click the dropdown arrow in the column "city."

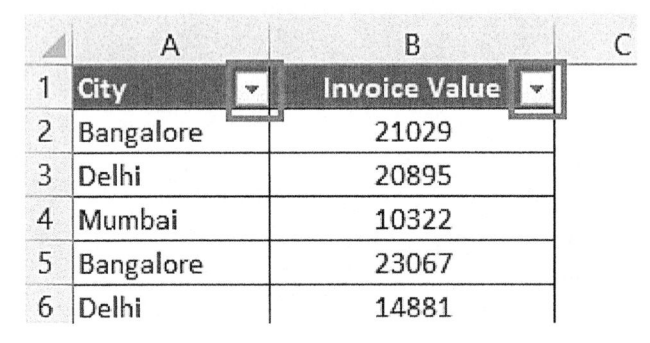

4. Select "Delhi" and uncheck all other boxes to get only the invoice values for "Delhi."

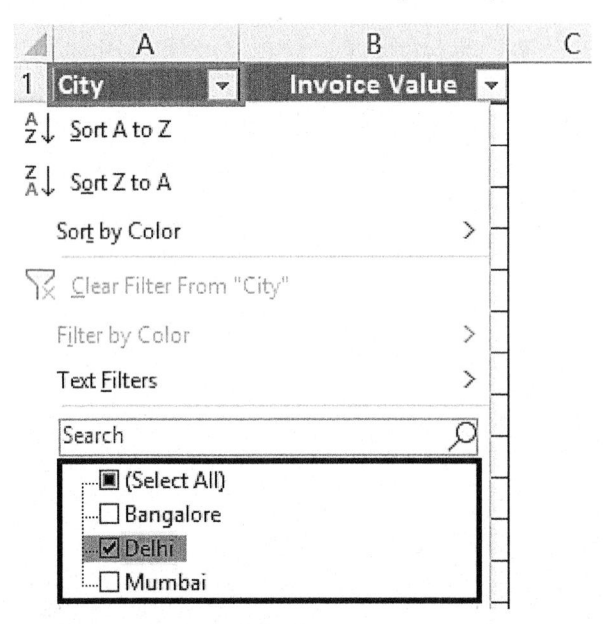

5. Filtered and showed statistics for the city of "Delhi."

	A	B	C
1	City	Invoice Value	
3	Delhi	20895	
6	Delhi	14881	
9	Delhi	23093	
13	Delhi	20891	
16	Delhi	10659	
17	Delhi	22827	
21			

Method 2:

Under the "sort and filter" area of the Data tab, select the "filter" option.

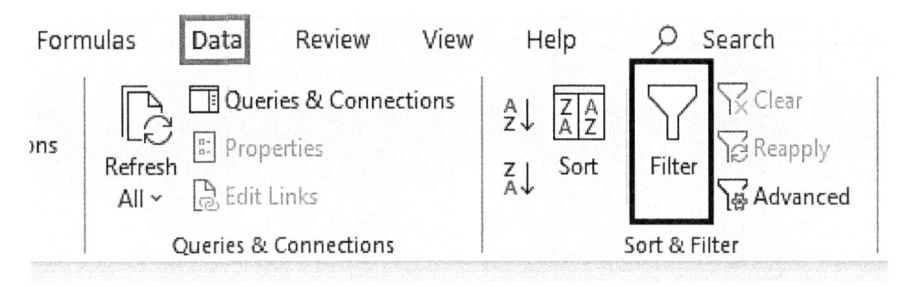

Method 3:

Keyboard shortcuts are a great method to make everyday tasks go faster. Using one of the shortcuts below, select the data and apply the filter:

Press the keys "Shift+Ctrl+L" at the same time.

5.10 How to Add Filters

Advanced strategies are used to filter numbers. Let's look at some examples to better grasp how Excel filters function:

Number Filters Option

Examples:
- To find integers larger than 10000 in column B (invoice value).

- To find numbers greater than 10000 but smaller than 20000 in column B, use the filter.

Use a filter with a number larger than 10000.

Step 1: Click on the filter symbol in column B (invoice value) to open the filter.

Step 2: In the "number filters" section, select "greater than," as seen in the image below.

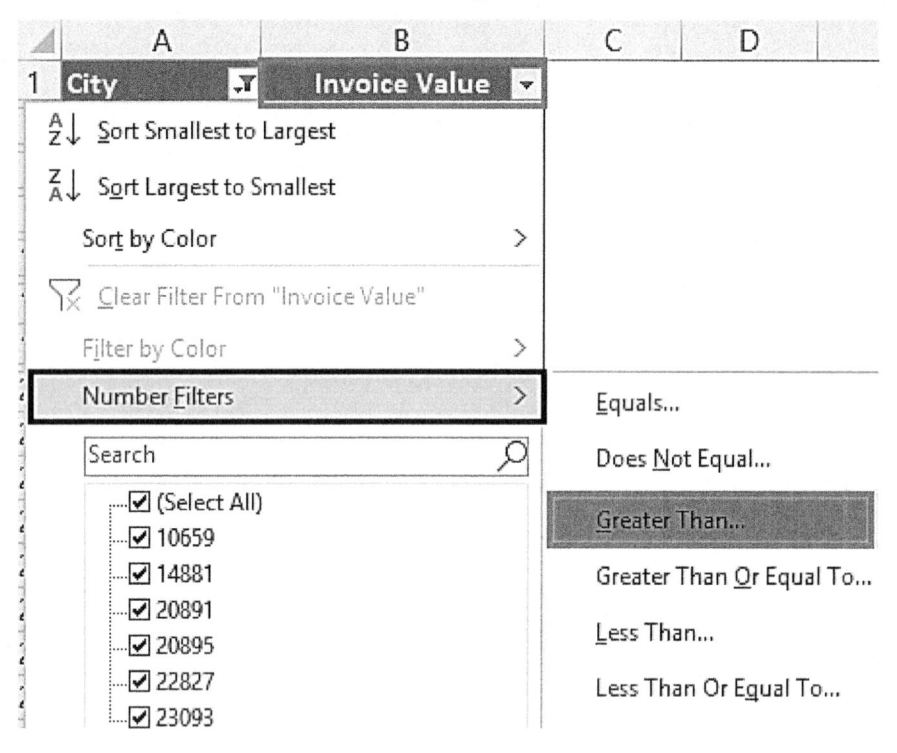

Step 3: A box called "custom auto-filter" appears.

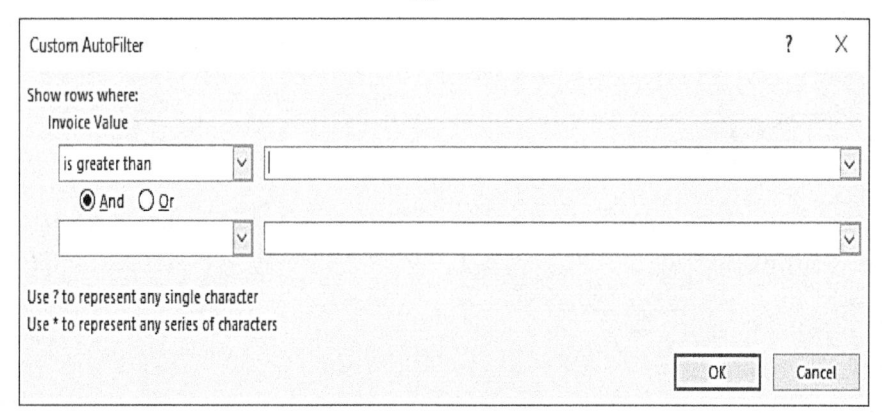

Step 4: In the box to the right of "is greater than," type 10000.

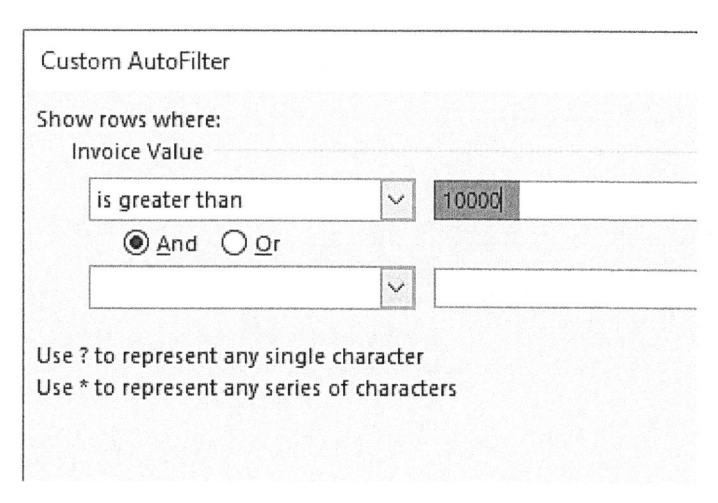

```
Custom AutoFilter

Show rows where:
    Invoice Value
        is greater than      ∨    10000
            ⦿ And   ○ Or
                             ∨

Use ? to represent any single character
Use * to represent any series of characters
```

Step 5: The invoice values larger than 10,000 are displayed in the output. The filter icon is the symbol within the red box.

	A	B	C
1	City	Invoice Value	
2	Bangalore	21029	
3	Delhi	20895	
4	Mumbai	10322	
5	Bangalore	23067	
6	Delhi	14881	
7	Mumbai	23383	
8	Bangalore	18390	
9	Delhi	23093	

And the filter has been applied to column B, as indicated.

Filter numbers larger than 10000 but fewer than 20000.

Step 1: Select "greater than" from the "number filters" menu.

Step 2: Select "is less than" in the second box on the left-hand side of the "custom auto filter" box.

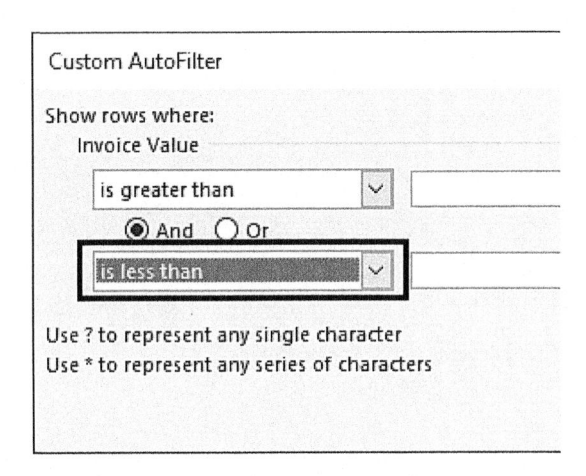

Step 3: In the box to the right of "is greater than," type 10000. In the box to the right of "is less than," type the number 20000.

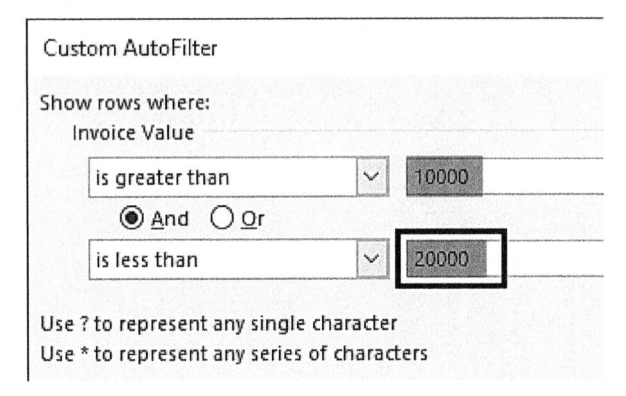

Step 4: The invoice values larger than 10,000 but less than 20,000 are displayed in the output.

	A	B
1	City	Invoice Value
4	Mumbai	10322
6	Delhi	14881
8	Bangalore	18390
10	Mumbai	11844
11	Bangalore	17722
12	Bangalore	10143
14	Mumbai	15335
15	Bangalore	18106
16	Delhi	10659
20	Bangalore	11431

"Search Box" Option:

Example:

For example, the first column (city) with product IDs is replaced while working on the data under the preceding item to filter the product ID "prd 1" 's details.

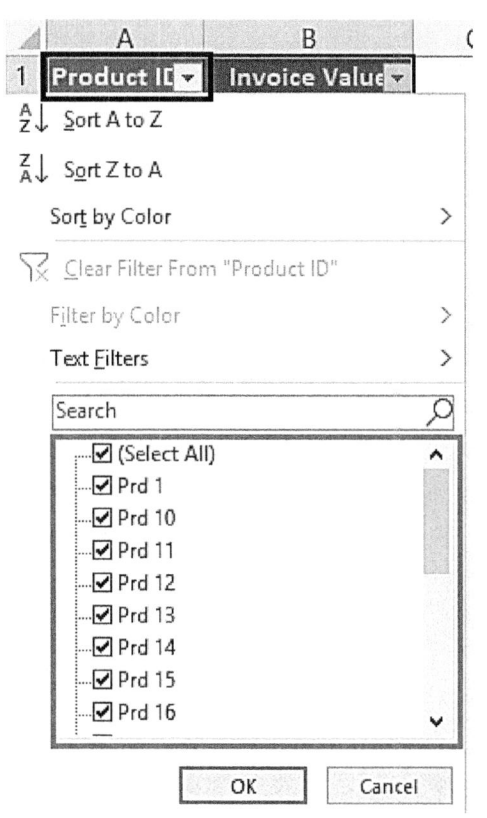

The following are the steps:

Step 1: Filter the columns "product ID" and "invoice value" with filters.

Step 2: Type the value to be filtered into the search box. So, type "prd 1" into the box.

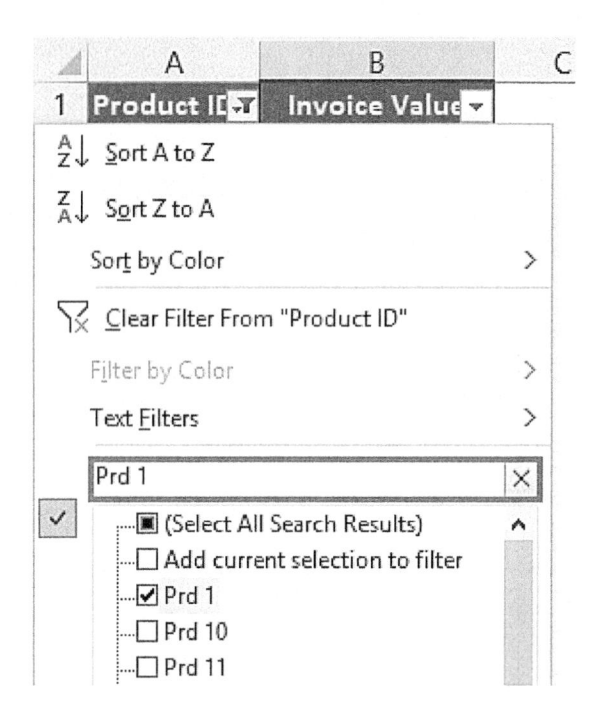

Step 3: As seen in the accompanying image, the output only shows the filtered value from the list. As a result, the billing value of the product ID "prd 1" may be shown.

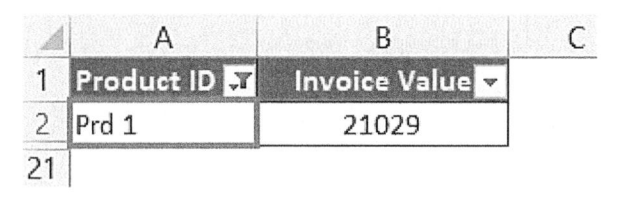

Text Filters

Text filters are used when you wish to filter a column by a specific word or number; when filter cells start or end with a specific character or text; when filter cells are based on whether or not they contain a specific character or word in the text.

When cells are identical to or not equivalent to a detailed character, text filters are used.

Example:

Let's say you wish to apply the filter on a single item.

1. Select equals from the text filter by clicking on it.

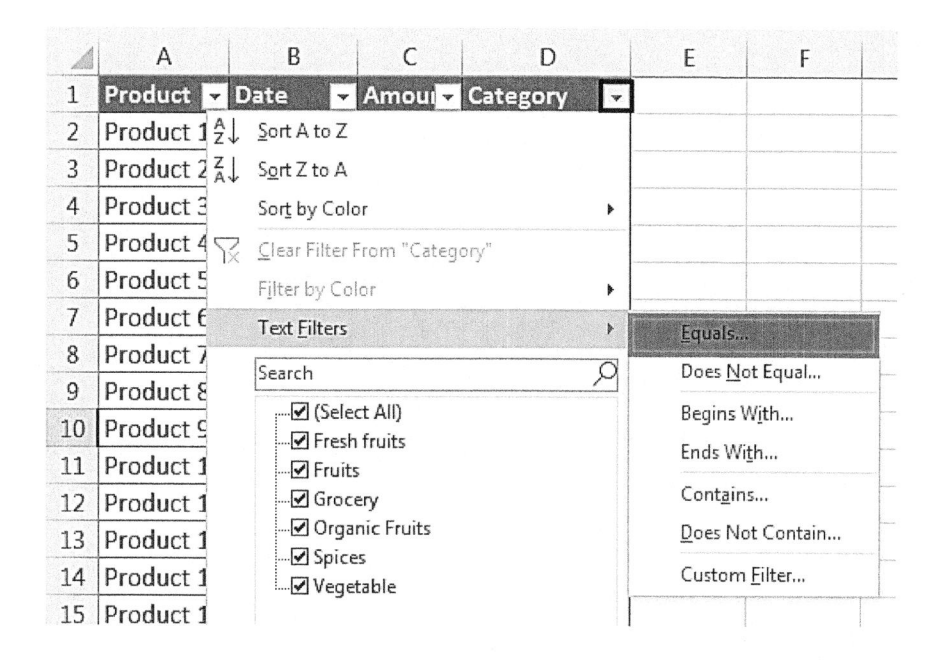

2. It gives you a single dialogue box with a Custom Auto-Filter dialogue box.

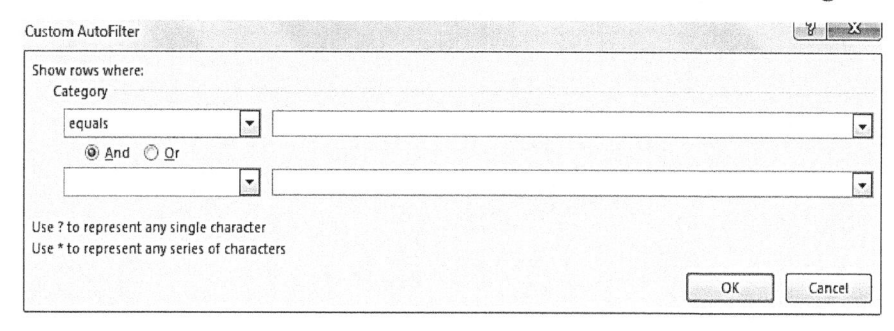

3. Select fruits from the dropdown menu and click OK.

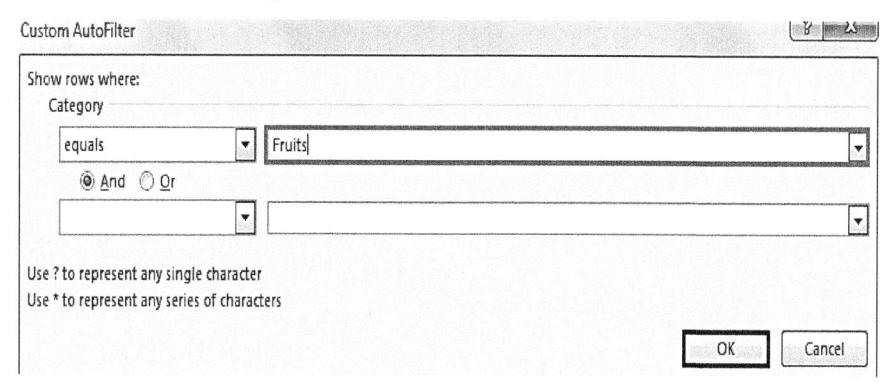

4. Now you'll only see data from the fruits category, as seen below.

	A	B	C	D	E
1	Product	Date	Amount	Category	
2	Product 1	12-Jun-18	477	Fruits	
9	Product 8	25-Nov-18	308	Fruits	
12	Product 11	28-Oct-18	553	Fruits	
13	Product 12	28-Oct-18	495	Fruits	
18	Product 17	15-Aug-18	592	Fruits	
22					

Colors can filter data if your data has rows with different colors or cells filled with different colors. Use the "Filter by Color" option.

DAY #4

"When you can not walk fast, walk. When you can't walk, use the cane. But never hold back!"

Madre Teresa of Calcutta

Chapter 6: Data Validation

Excel Data Validation is a feature that prevents (validates) users from entering data into a spreadsheet. In technical terms, you define a validation rule limiting the types of data entered into a cell.

Excel data validation helps to control the data that is entered into your worksheet. Excel data validation, for example, allows you to limit data entries to a dropdown list selection and restrict specific data entries, such as dates or integers, to a predetermined range. Data validation can also aid in the control of formulas and the data they generate.

You can create custom Excel data validation alerts when users reach a limit to lead them to the correct data entry. As a result, Excel data validation aids in the reduction of unstandardized data, inaccuracies, and unnecessary data in your spreadsheet.

It's a useful function, especially when working on an Excel worksheet with many people. When working with a large number of users or rigorous data entry rules, many data analysts find Excel data validation useful. Furthermore, Excel data validation can help analysts save time and money by entering data correctly. Overall, Excel's data validation is a useful function, but even useful features have restrictions limiting their capacity to assist users.

Data-validation methods are a fantastic line of defense against careless data entry and that itch you get when you're stuck on a tedious task. You can require dates to fall within a specified time limit in a cell that records date entries. You can select an item from a list rather than typing it yourself in a cell that records text entries. You can require a number to fall inside a specified range in a cell that records numeric entries. Here are a few instances of what data validation in Excel can do:

- In a cell, only numeric or text values are permitted.
- Allow only numbers that fall within a certain range.
- Allow for a certain number of characters in each data entry.
- Dates and times outside of a specified range are restricted.
- Restrict entries to a dropdown list of options.
- Validate an entry using information from another cell.
- When the user picks a cell, display an input message.
- When erroneous data is entered, display a warning message.
- Invalid entries will be in invalidated cells.

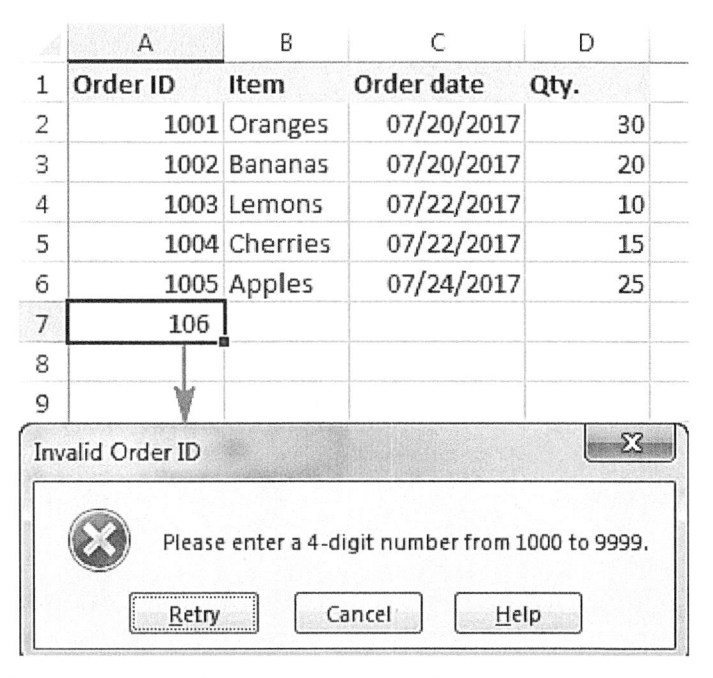

	A	B	C	D
1	Order ID	Item	Order date	Qty.
2	1001	Oranges	07/20/2017	30
3	1002	Bananas	07/20/2017	20
4	1003	Lemons	07/22/2017	10
5	1004	Cherries	07/22/2017	15
6	1005	Apples	07/24/2017	25
7	106			
8				
9				

Invalid Order ID

Please enter a 4-digit number from 1000 to 9999.

[Retry] [Cancel] [Help]

You can, for example, create a rule that restricts data entry to four-digit figures between 1000 and 9999. If the user inputs something else, Excel will display an error message detailing what went wrong.

6.1 How to Validate Data in Excel

Follow the instructions below to add data validation to Excel:

1. Click the Validate Data button in the Data Validation dialogue box.

2. Select 1 or more cells to validate, then click the Data Validation button on the Data tab > Data Tools group.

3. Alternatively, you can access the Data Validation dialogue box by hitting Alt > D > L, one key at a time.

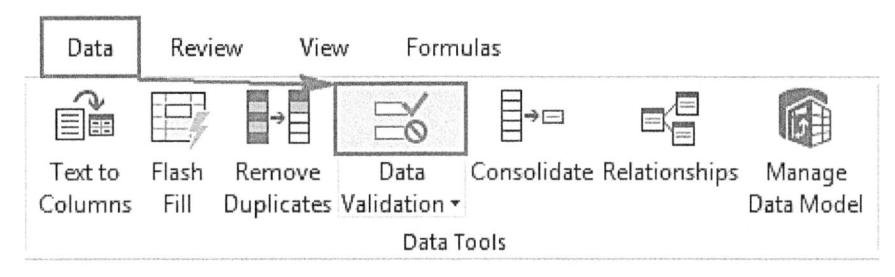

6.2 How to make a validation rule in Excel

Specify the validation criteria on the Settings tab according to your requirements:

- Values – fill in the criteria boxes with numbers, as indicated in the screenshot below.
- Make a rule depending on a value or formula in another cell using cell references.
- Formulas – enable the expression of more complicated conditions, such as those in this example.

You want to build a rule that only allows users to enter whole numbers between 1000 and 9999.

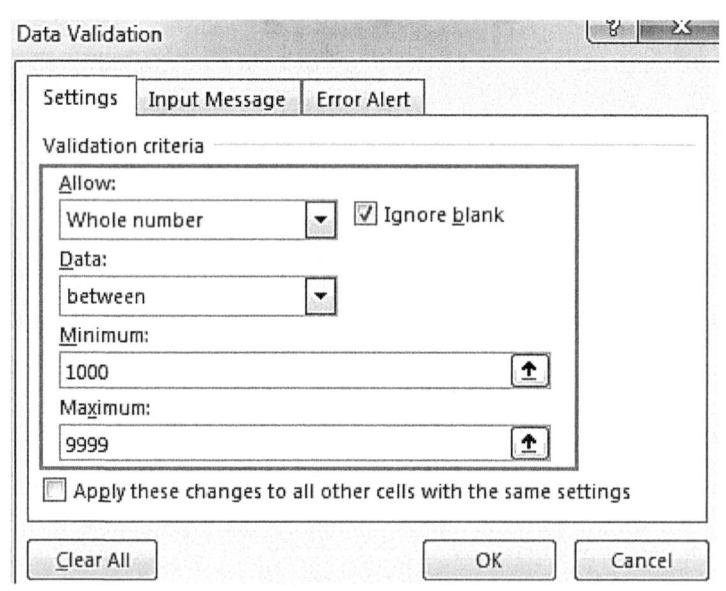

After you've set up the validation rule, click OK to leave the Data Validation window or navigate to another tab to include an input message or error warning.

6.3 List of Excel data validations (dropdown)

Select the target cells and perform the following steps to add a dropdown list of items to them:

1. Open the Data Validation dialogue box in the Data tab.
2. Select List in the Allow box on the Settings tab.
3. Type the elements from your Excel validation list in the Source box, separated by commas. Type Yes, No, and N/A to limit the user input to three options.

4. To see the dropdown arrow next to the cell, ensure the In-cell dropdown box is chosen.

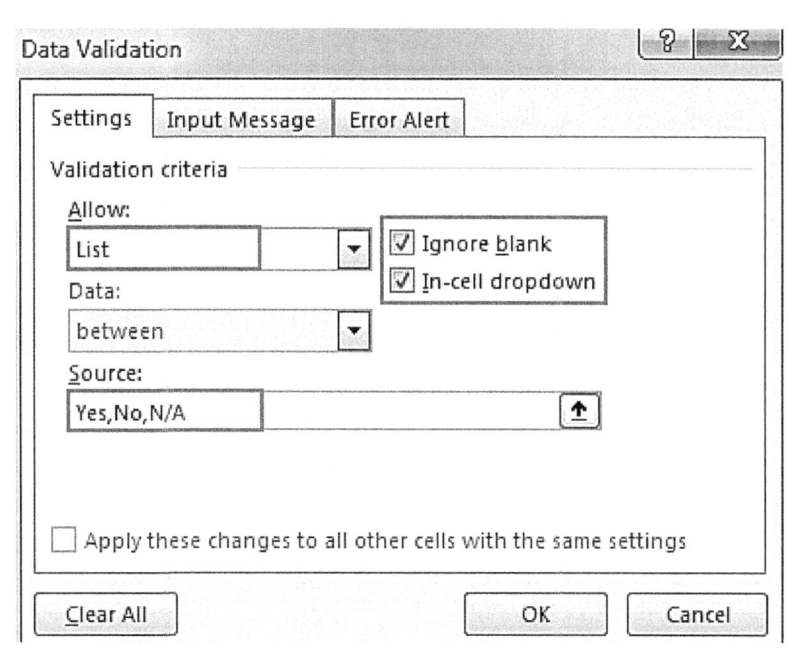

5. Click the OK button.

The Excel data validation list that results will look somewhat like this:

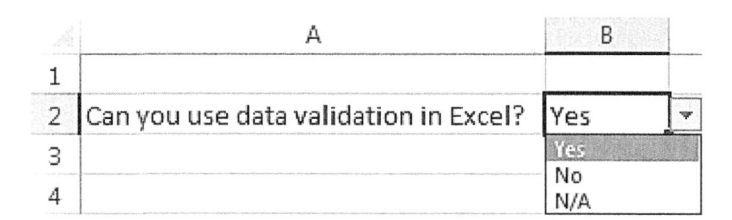

There are a few other ways to make a data validation list in Excel.

The quickest method for short dropdowns that are unlikely to change is to enter comma-separated lists directly in the Source box. In other cases, you can take one of the following approaches:

- From a set of cells, create a data validation list.
- Using a designated range, create a dynamic data validation list.
- From the table, create an Excel data validation list. The nicest part is that a table-based dropdown is by its very nature dynamic, updating itself as you delete or add items from the table.

6.4 Copy Excel data validation rule for other cells

Sometimes one cell is configured with validation, and you want to apply the same validation to other cells. For that, you do not need to do it from the beginning. To validate other cells with the same criteria, do the following:

1. Select any cell on which validation rule had been applied and then copy it by right-clicking and selecting the copy option.
2. Then select other cells to apply validation.
3. If the cells are non-adjacent, to select them, press and hold the Ctrl key while selecting the cells.
4. Right-click on them.
5. Click Paste Special
6. Select the Validation option.
7. Click OK.

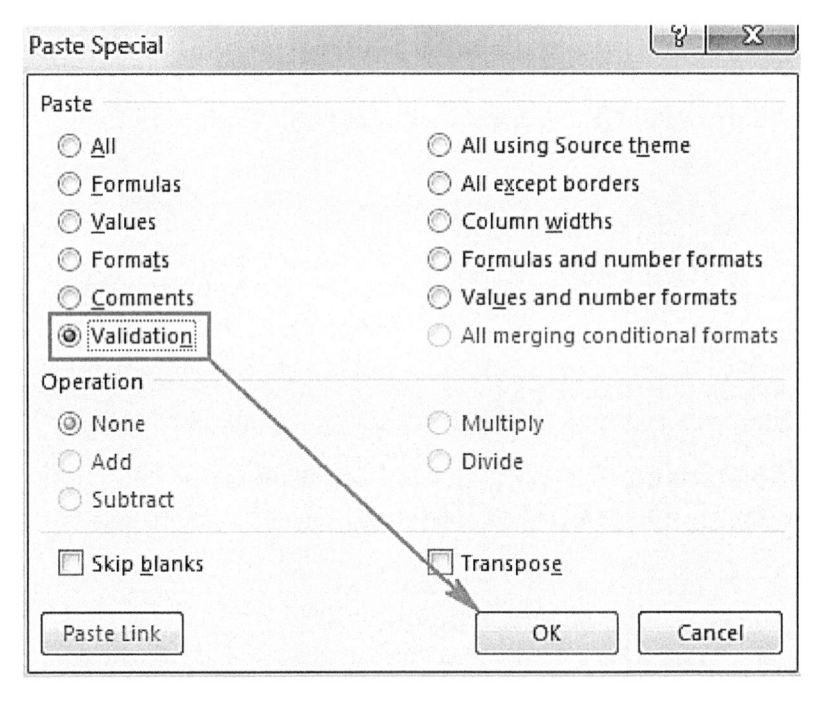

6.5 How to remove data validation

Overall, there are two methods for removing validation in Excel: the Microsoft-designed method and the mouse-free method invented by Excel nerds.

Method 1: The traditional method of removing data validation

To eliminate data validation in Excel worksheets, typically follow these steps:

1. Choose the cell(s) that require data confirmation.
2. Go to the Data Tab of the Ribbon click the Data Validation command.
3. Click the Clear All button on the Settings tab, then click OK.

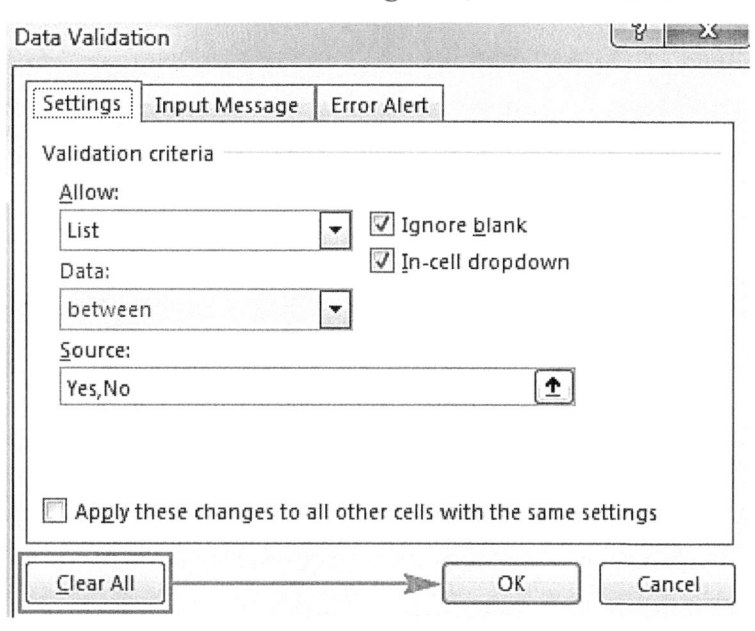

Method 2: Delete data validation rules using Paste Special

Excel Paste Special is intended for pasting certain elements of copied cells, according to the law. In reality, it's capable of a lot more. It can, for example, rapidly remove data validation rules from a worksheet. Here's how to do it:

1. Select any empty cell with no data validation and copy it with Ctrl + C.
2. Select the cell(s) to remove data validation.
3. The shortcut for Data Validation is Ctrl + Alt + V, then N.
4. Enter the code.

Here are some tips for data validation:

- Use the Find & Select function to select all of the validated cells on the current sheet to remove data validation from all of them.
- Select any cell with a data validation rule, open the Data Validation dialogue window
- Click the Apply these changes to all of the other cells with the same settings checkbox, and then hit the Clear All button to remove it.

Chapter 7: Formatting Cells

In Excel, you can modify the font, font size, font style, and font color of cells and their contents, add cell borders and change the background color of cells. You can format a cell before entering data or entering the data since formatting is related to the cell rather than the entry.

The most used formatting commands are found in the font group on the "Home tab" of the Ribbon. The following is a collection of topics that describe how to use Excel cells.

7.1 Change the Font

To improve your document, you can change the font in any cell.

To adjust the font in a cell, first, pick the text you need to alter. It can be the entire cell or just a single character within it. By default, the font in Excel is Calibri.

7.2 To adjust the font of your data

1. Choose the Cell or Cells.
2. Select any new font from the Font group drop-down arrow in the Home Tab of the Ribbon.

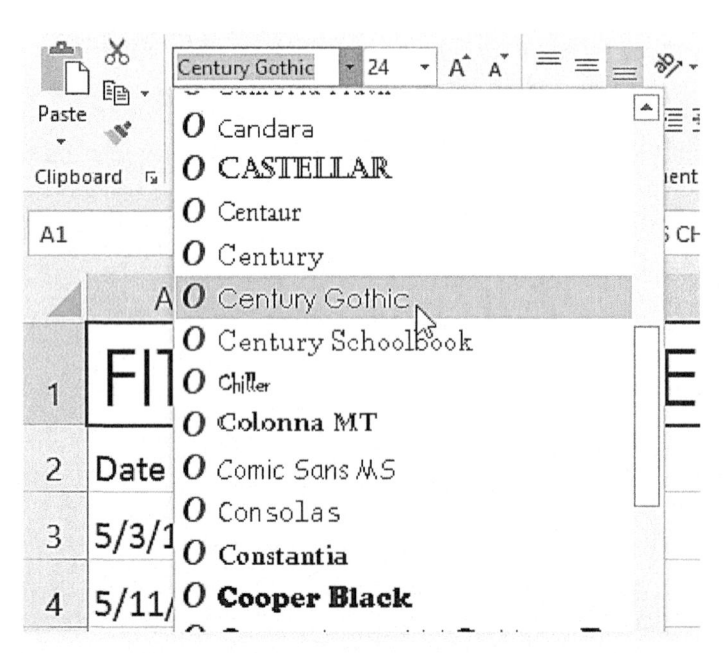

7.3 To adjust the font size of your data

1. Select the Cell or Cells.
2. Click the Font Size arrow in the Font group on the Home menu.
3. Then select the font size from the menu.
4. If the font size you want isn't included in the Font Size list, type the number in the Font Size field and press the Enter key.
5. You can also utilize the increasing or decreasing font size commands or use your keyboard to change the font size.

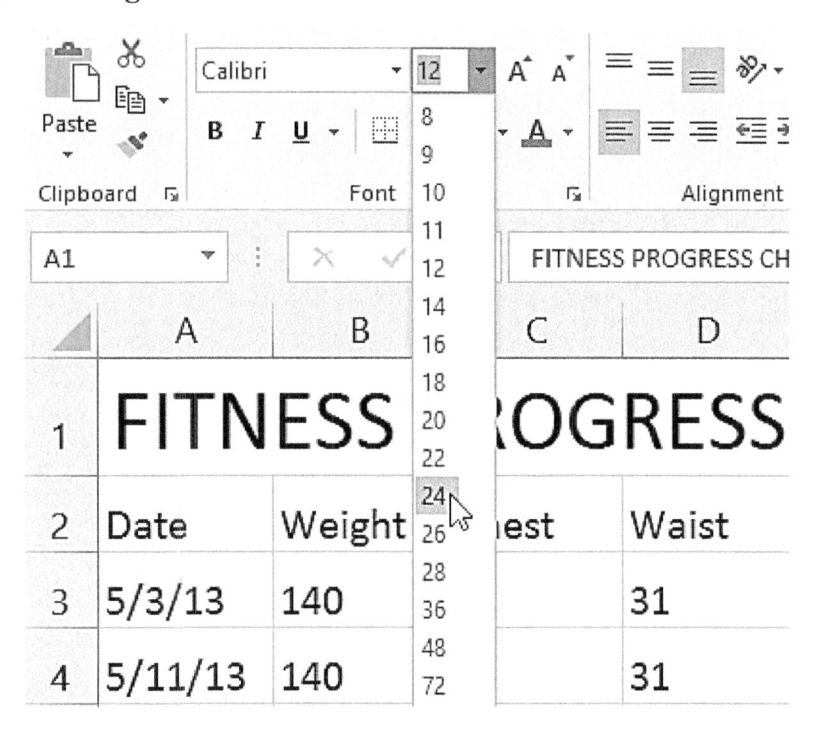

7.4 To modify the font color

1. Choose the Cell or Cells.
2. On the Home tab, click the desired font color by clicking the drop-down menu next to the Font Color function.
3. It will change the text color.
4. To see more color options, go to the bottom of that menu and select More Colors.

Bold, Italic, and Underline functions in the Font group of the Home Tab can also be used. The selected styled will be applied to the desired text.

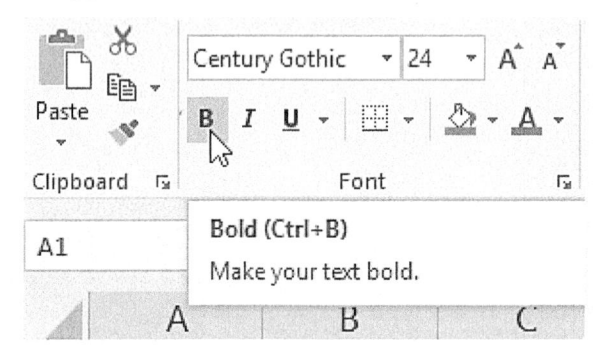

7.5 Cell Alignment

Text typed into your worksheet will be oriented to the bottom-left of a cell by default, while numbers are aligned to the bottom right. Modifying the alignment of your cell content allows you to customize how the material in each cell is displayed, making it easier to read.

The way the text interacts with the available space in the cell is referred to as cell alignment. The direction of the text is referred to as orientation.

Text runs horizontally from left to right by default. The Orientation button on the Home tab of the Ribbon is used to modify this. You could use vertical or diagonal text, for example, to make labels in a header row take up less horizontal space.

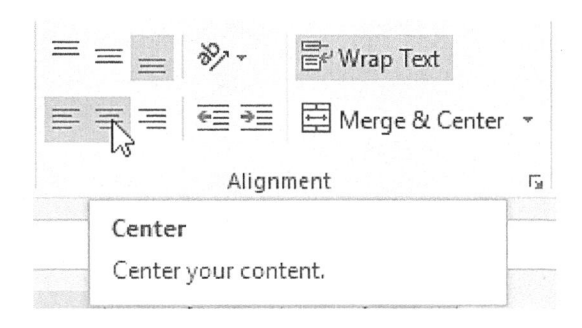

- Select the cell (s), click the Orientation button and choose an option from the menu.
- When the cell is bigger than needed to hold the entry, horizontal orientation indicates whether the text is left-aligned, right-aligned, or centered.
- Vertical orientation refers to whether the text aligns with the top or bottom of the cell or is balanced vertically between the top and bottom when the cell is larger than required to handle the input. If you need a more dramatic text alignment, the Degrees field allows you to rotate cell content 90 degrees up or down in either direction.

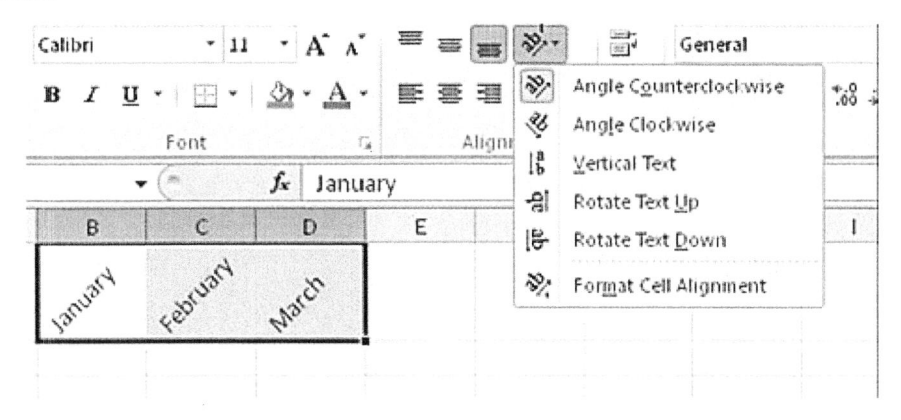

Text Control is also used to change the way Excel formats data in a cell. Wrapped text, compress to fit, and combine cells are the three methods of text control.

Finally, Text Direction changes the worksheet's direction—in other words, column A may begin on the upper right side rather than the upper left:

1. To make any of these changes, first, choose the text you'd like to change.
2. Select the option of Format, then Format Cells from the Home tab.
3. Format Cells dialogue box will appear.

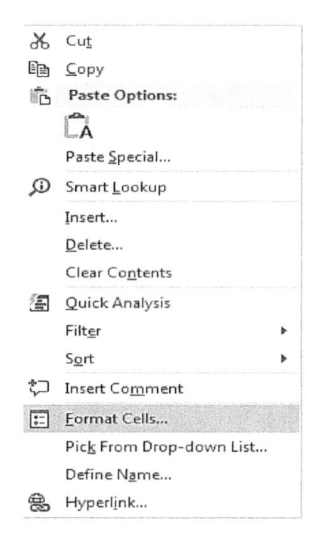

4. Select the Alignment tab from the drop-down menu.

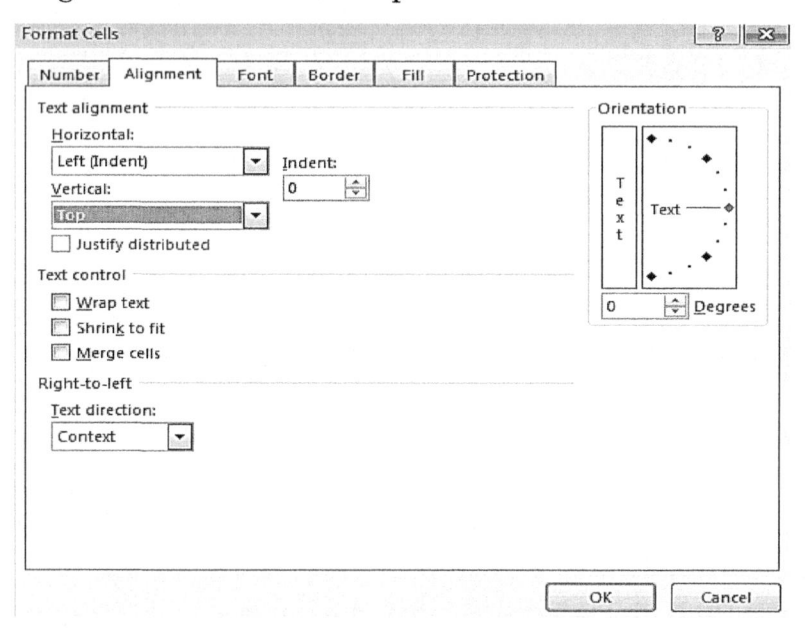

5. Text Alignment Horizontal or Vertical, Text Control with Wrap text, Shrink to Fit, Merge cells, and Text Direction is all available from there.

7.6 Adding borders and Fill colors in a cell

You may establish obvious and defined boundaries into different sections of your worksheet using cell borders and fill colors. To further identify our header cells from the rest of the worksheet, we'll add cell borders and fill color to them.

Add borders around a single cell or a range of cells. To add border:

1. Select the cell you want to apply a border.
2. Click on the Border command in the Font group of the Home Tab.
3. Click the Borders arrow to choose a new border from the menu.

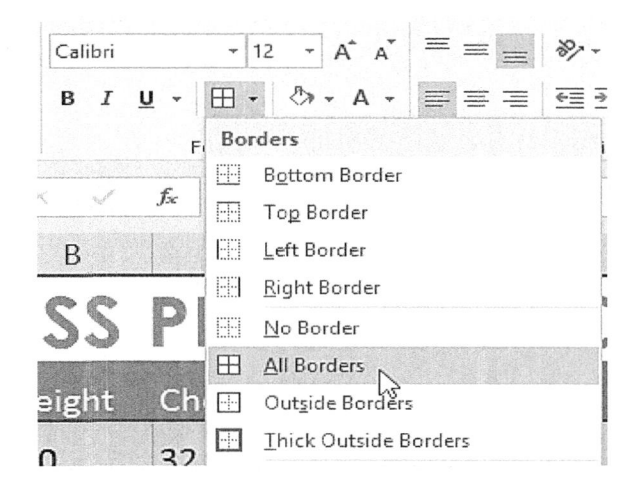

To fill color:

1. Select the cell
2. Click on the Fill Color command in the Font group of Home tab of Ribbon.
3. Select the color
4. The fill color you choose will show in the cells you choose.
5. Choose a variety of other colors from more colors options.

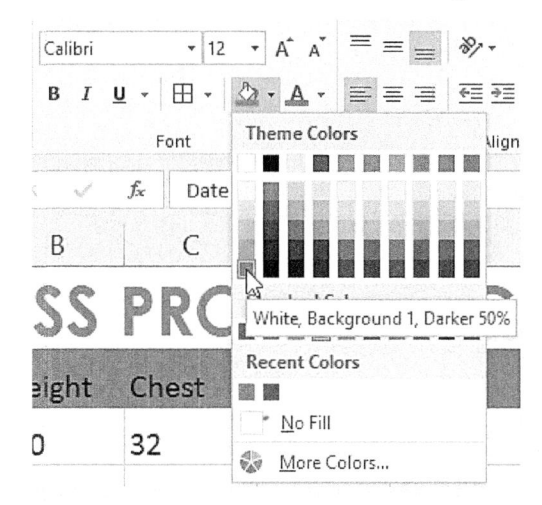

7.7 Formatting Text and Numbers

Number formats can be added to cells to better reflect the sort of data they represent. You can show a numeric value as a percentage, currency, date or time, and so forth. The most commonly used commands for formatting numbers are found in the Number group on the "Home tab" of the Ribbon. Click on the dialogue box launcher to format numbers.

Using the icons on the Formatting tab, you may apply a variety of numerical formats to cells. To change the number format, click the cell and then click the appropriate icon.

Use the Numbers page of the Format Cells dialogue for greater control or to select different number formats:

1. Choose the cell that has to be formatted.
2. Select the Accounting Number option from the "Home Tab" in the Number group.
3. It is General by default.
4. Click the Format button to show the integer with a dollar sign, comma separators, and up to two decimal places.
5. Select Percent Style from the drop-down menu to change a number into a percentage and show it using a graph.
6. To display the value with comma separators and 2 decimal places, click the Comma Style button.

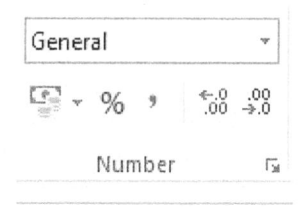

To change the number of decimal places:

1. Choose the cell that has to be edited.
2. In the Number group on the "Home tab." Click on the small boxes of decimals.
3. Increase the number of decimals by clicking the Increase Decimal button.
4. To reduce the number of decimal places, click the Decrease Decimal option.

DAY #5

"I'm convinced that about half of what separates successful entrepreneurs from the non-successful ones is pure perseverance"

Steve Jobs

Chapter 8: Formulas and Functions

This chapter discusses formulas and functions. What is the formula for how to use it with examples? What are functions, their types and examples?

8.1 Formula

A formula in Excel is the argument that works with values in a single cell or range of cells. Cell A3 beneath, for example, has a formula that sums the number of cell A2 to the value of cell A1.

8.2 To enter the formula

Follow the instructions below to enter a formula:

1. Pick a cell to work with.
2. Type an equal symbol (=) to tell Excel you want to input a formula.

3. Type the formula A1+A2 as an example.
4. Change cell A1's value to 3.
5. Excel automatically regenerates the value of cell A3.

84

8.3 To Edit Formula

Excel displays the value or formula of a cell in the formula bar when you click it:

1. To update a formula, click on the formula bar and make the necessary changes.
2. Hit the Enter key.

By Operator Priority

The order by which computations are performed in Excel is set by default. If a section of the formula is included in parenthesis, it will be computed first. After that, it calculates multiplication and division. When you're through, Excel will add and subtract the rest of your formula. Take a look at the sample below.

Excel starts by multiplying the numbers (A1 * A2). The value of cell A3 is then added to this result by Excel.

	A	B	C	D	E	F
1	2					
2	2					
3	1					
4	6					
5						

A4 — fx =A1*(A2+A3)

8.4 Make a Formula by Copy/Paste

Excel automatically updates the cell references for every cell the formula is copied to when you copy a formula. Execute the actions below to gain a better understanding of this.

1. In cell A4, write the formula indicated below.

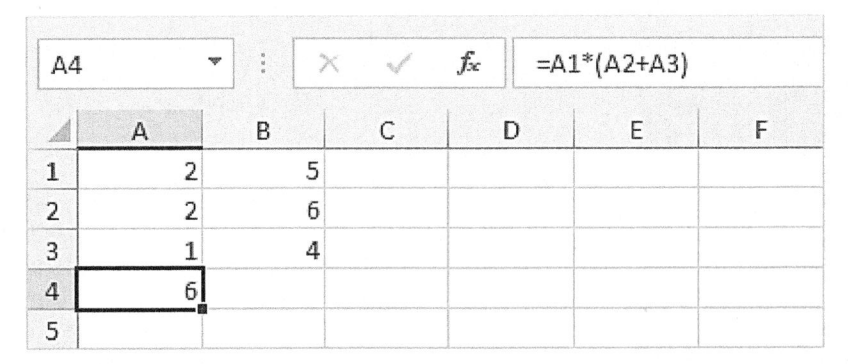

A4 — fx =A1*(A2+A3)

	A	B	C	D	E	F
1	2	5				
2	2	6				
3	1	4				
4	6					
5						

2a. Select cell A4, right-click, and then select Copy and Paste from the 'Paste Options' menu.

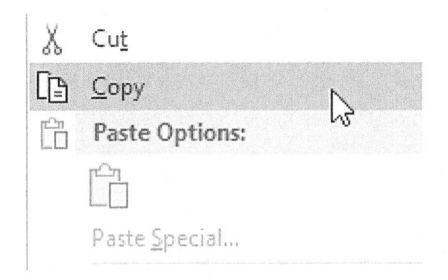

- Cut
- Copy
- Paste Options:
- Paste Special...

2b. you may also move the formula to cell B4 by dragging it there. Cell A4 is selected, and the lower right corner of cell A4 is clicked and dragged over to cell B4. It is a lot easier and produces the same outcome!

Result. The formula references the numbers in column B in cell B4.

The Dollar Sign ($) in Excel Formula

Excel's most helpful feature is the ability to connect to cells or ranges and use them in computations. When you replicate these formulae, the cell references may change automatically. You begin employing the Dollar signs in your Excel calculation when you use Absolute References. The dollar signs instruct Excel to fix a specific element of a cell's location and prevent it from altering when you drag or copy the formula to other cells. There are three ways to change the placement of a cell.

= $A1

As the Dollar sign appears before the Column letter A, Column A is the fixed-point. This formula will always refer back to Column A if copied or dragged anyplace else on the spreadsheet. Depending on where the formula is copied, the Row will differ.

= A$1

because the Dollar sign appears before Row number 1, Row 1 is the fixed point. This formula will always refer back to Row 1 if copied or dragged anyplace else on the spreadsheet. Depending on where the formula is duplicated, the Column will change.

= $A$1 because there is a Dollar sign before the column letter and the Row Number, Cell A1 is the fixed-point. This formula will always refer to Cell A1, whether copying or moving it on the Excel page.

Example:

When you use a $ sign before a cell reference (for example, $C$2), Excel will continue to refer to cell C3 even if you copy and paste the formula.

The dollar ($) sign can now be used in three different ways, indicating three different sorts of references in Excel.

| C2 | | | fx | =A2+B2 |

	A	B	C	D
1	Col 1	Col 2	Col1 + Col2	
2	36	39	75	
3	73	37		
4	70	36		
5	73	26		
6	14	30		
7				

| C3 | | | fx | |

	A	B	C	D
1	Col 1	Col 2	Col1 + Col2	
2	36	39	75	
3	73	37		
4	70	36		
5	73	26		
6	14	30		
7				

	A	B	C	D
1	Col 1	Col 2	Col1 + Col2	
2	36	39	75	
3	73	37	110	
4	70	36		
5	73	26		
6	14	30		
7				

C3: =A3+B3

8.5 Add Formula Using Insert Function Key

You can use the Insert Function command on the Formula bar to use other Excel functions (the one with the fx). Excel displays the Insert Function dialogue box when you click the Insert Function button. Then, you can utilize its options to locate and pick the function you wish to employ and define the argument or arguments the function requires to execute its calculations.

The structure of each function is the same SUM, for example (A1:A4). SUM is the name of this function. The part within the brackets (arguments) indicates that we are giving Excel the range A1:A4. The values in cells A1, A2, A3, and A4 are added using this function.

Execute the steps below to insert a function:

1. Select a cell.

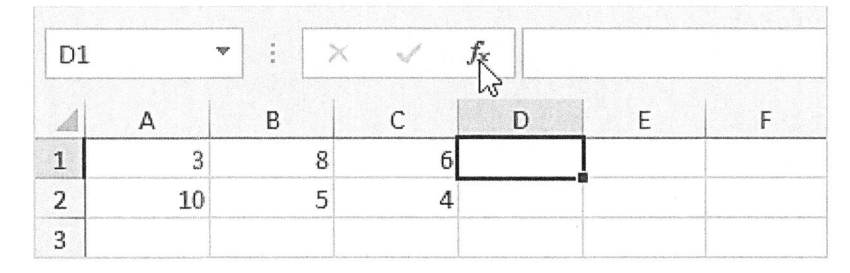

	A	B	C	D	E	F
1	3	8	6			
2	10	5	4			
3						

2. Select Insert Function from the drop-down menu. The dialogue window for 'Insert Function' appears.

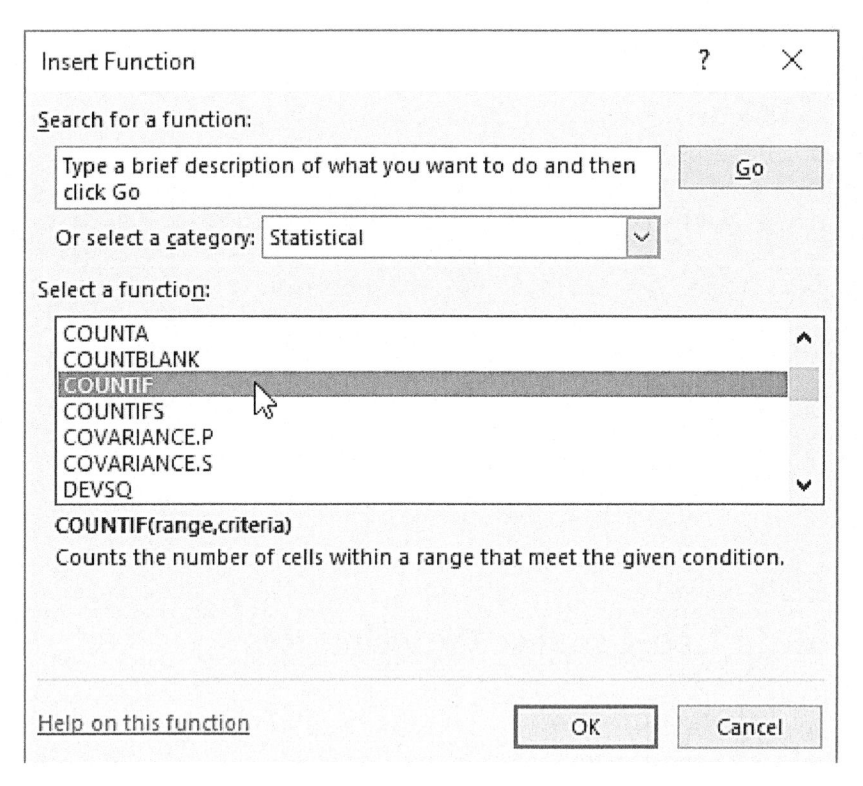

3. Look for a function or choose one from a category. Choose COUNTIF from the Statistical category, for example.

4. Select OK.

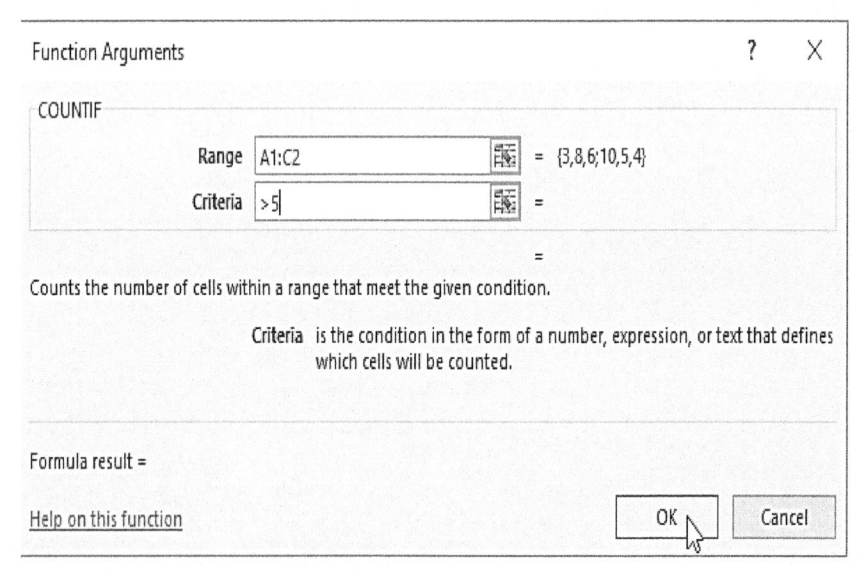

5. The dialogue box for 'Function Arguments' appears.

6. Select the A1:C2 range in the Range box by clicking on it.

7. Type >5 in the Criteria box and click OK.

8. COUNTIF counts the number of cells in a row that are bigger than 5.

D1			f_x	=COUNTIF(A1:C2,">5")	
	A	B	C	D	E	F
1	3	8	6	3		
2	10	5	4			
3						

8.6 How to use formula?

There are three ways to use the formula:

- Inserting basic Excel formulas is as simple as typing a formula in a cell or using the formula bar. Typically, the procedure begins with an equal sign followed by the name of an Excel function. Excel is clever in that it displays a pop-up function indication as you start typing the function name. You'll choose your preference from this list.

- You can use the Insert Function command to look for functions using keywords. This command, while helpful, can be challenging to use at times. Choose the Insert Function icon to open the Insert Function dialogue box (same dialogue box as the previous way), click the arrow next to the appropriate category in the Function Library Group, and then choose the intended functions. The Insert Function dialogue box that appears displays a list of Excel's capabilities. Choose a category from "choose a category" (which includes a "display all" option) and then a specific function from "Select a function."

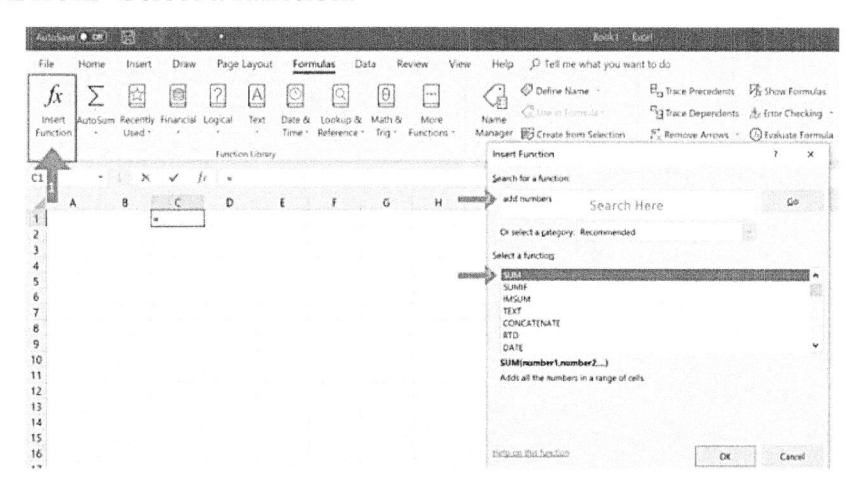

- And AutoSum function is a tool for quick and everyday jobs. So, go to the Home tab and choose the AutoSum option in the far-right corner. Then press the mouse cursor to reveal more formulas that were previously concealed. This option is also available in the Formulas tab.

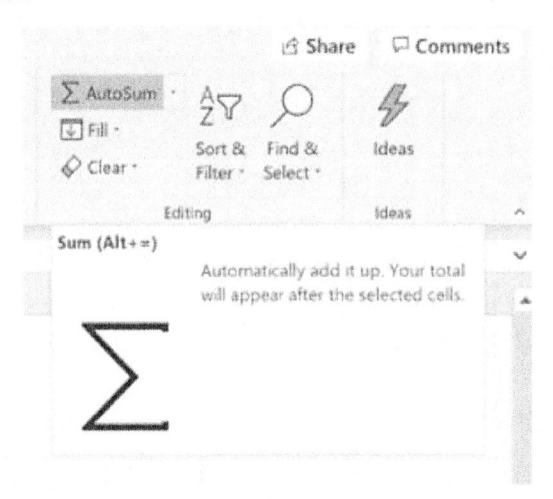

8.7 Functions

In Excel, functions are basically predefined formulas.

=SUM, for example (A1:A3). The function adds up all of the values in the range A1 to A3.

8.7.1 Number Functions

Here are some commonly used Number Functions in Excel:

1. **SUM**

The SUM function in Microsoft Excel adds all the integers in a range of cells and returns the result. The SUM function is an arithmetic function that comes standard with Excel.

Syntax: SUM (number1, [number2, ... number_n])

Example:

	A	B	C	D	E	F	G
1	Value						
2	10.5		17.7				
3	7.2						
4	200						
5	5.4						
6	8.1						

C2, f_x =SUM(A2, A3)

=SUM (A2, A3) Result is 17.7

2. AVERAGE

When using the AVERAGE function, a simple average of data, such as the average number of investors in a certain shareholding pool, should come to mind.

Syntax: AVERAGE (number1, [number2],…)

Example:

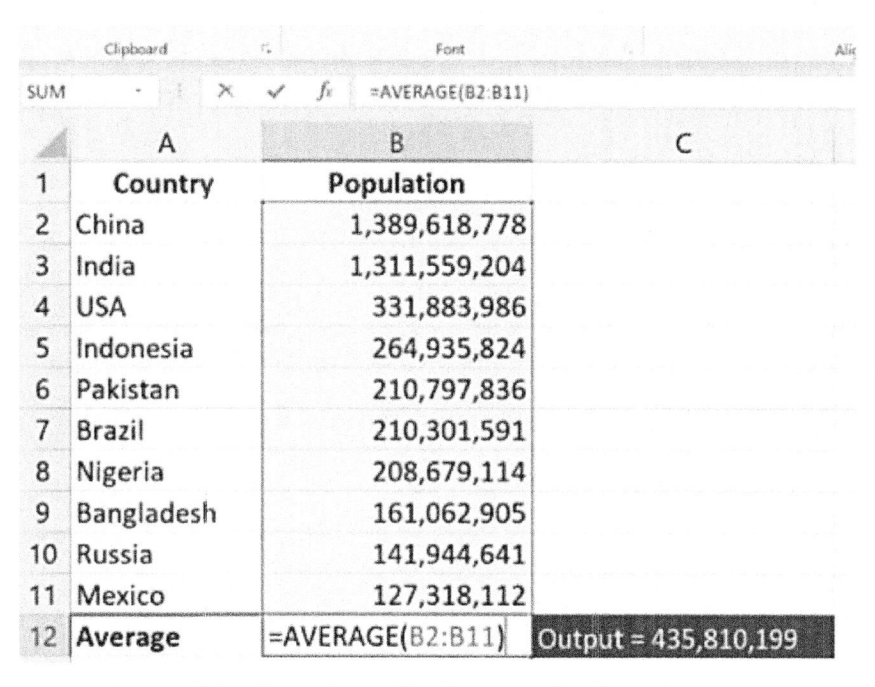

	A	B
1	Country	Population
2	China	1,389,618,778
3	India	1,311,559,204
4	USA	331,883,986
5	Indonesia	264,935,824
6	Pakistan	210,797,836
7	Brazil	210,301,591
8	Nigeria	208,679,114
9	Bangladesh	161,062,905
10	Russia	141,944,641
11	Mexico	127,318,112
12	Average	=AVERAGE(B2:B11) Output = 435,810,199

=AVERAGE (B2:B11) – This function displays a basic average, equivalent to (SUM (B2:B11)/10).

3. SUMIF

The SUMIF function in Excel sums all integers in a range of cells based on a single criterion (for example, it is equal to 2000).

The SUMIF function in Excel is a built-in function that may also be used as a worksheet function.

Example:

	A	B	C	D	E	F	G
1	Year	Date	Value	Criteria		218.6	
2	2000	8/1/2000	10.5	2000			
3	2003	5/12/2003	7.2				
4	2000	3/12/2000	200				
5	2001	7/30/2001	5.4				
6	2000	2/28/2000	8.1				

F1: =SUMIF(A2:A6, D2, C2:C6)

To see named ranges, go to the toolbar at the top of the screen, select the Formulas tab. Then, in the Defined Names group, select Name Manager from the Defined Names drop-down menu.

The window for the Name Manager should now appear.

4. RUNDOWN

The ROUNDDOWN function in Microsoft Excel produces a number that has been rounded down to a specified number of digits. (Always round to the nearest tenth.)

The ROUNDDOWN function is an Excel built-in function that is classified as a Number Function.

Syntax: ROUNDDOWN (number, digits)

Example:

ROUNDDOWN (A1, 0)

Result: 662

	A	B	C	D	E	F	G
1	662.79		662				
2	54.1						
3							
4							
5							
6							

C1: =ROUNDDOWN(A1, 0)

5. ROUNDUP

The ROUNDUP function in Microsoft Excel produces a number that has been rounded up to a specified number of digits.

The ROUNDUP function is a built-in function in Excel that is categorized as a number

Function.

Syntax: ROUNDUP (number, digits)

Example:

	A	B	C	D	E	F	G
1	662.79		663				
2	54.1						
3							
4							
5							
6							

C1 = =ROUNDUP(A1, 0)

ROUNDUP (A1, 0)

Result: 663

6. SUMPRODUCT

The SUMPRODUCT function in Microsoft Excel multiplies the items in the arrays and returns the sum of the results. The SUMPRODUCT function is an Excel built-in function that is classified as a Number Function.

Syntax: SUMPRODUCT (array1, [array2, ... array_n])

Example:

	A	B	C	D	E
1	1	2		5	6
2	3	4		7	8
3					
4					
5					
6					

A1 = 1

Example: =SUMPRODUCT (A1:B2, D1:E2)

Result is 70

7. ROUND

The ROUND function in Microsoft Excel returns a number that has been rounded to a given number of digits. The ROUND function is an Excel built-in function that is classified as a Math Function.

Example:

	A	B	C	D	E	F	G
1	662.79		663				
2	54.1						
3							
4							
5							
6							

C1: =ROUND(A1, 0)

=ROUND (A1, 0) 663

8. POWER

The POWER function in Microsoft Excel returns the result of raising a number to a specific power. The POWER function is an Excel built-in function that is categorized as a Math Function.

Example:

	A	B	C	D	E	F	G
1	3		81				
2	4						
3	4.5						
4							
5							
6							

C1: =POWER(A1, A2)

The following POWER samples would be returned based on the Excel file above:

The result of =POWER (A1, A2) is 81.

9. SQRT

The SQRT function in Microsoft Excel calculates the square root of an integer. The SQRT function is an Excel built-in function that is classified as a Number Function.

Syntax: SQRT (number)

Example:

	A	B	C	D	E	F	G
1	25		5				
2	33.6						
3	-5.2						
4							
5							
6							

C1 — fx =SQRT(A1)

=SQRT (A1)

Result is 5

8.7.2 Text Functions

Here are some commonly used Text Functions:

1. T

The T function in Microsoft Excel returns the text referenced to by a value. The T function is an Excel built-in function that is classified as a Text Function. The T function can be used as part of a formula in a worksheet cell.

Syntax: T (value)

Example:

C1 — fx =T(A1)

	A	B	C	D	E	F
1	Alphabet soup		Alphabet soup			
2	techonthenet					
3	34 hats					
4	567					
5	techonthenet.com					
6						

The following T samples would be returned focusing on the Excel spreadsheet above:

=T (A1) Result is "Alphabet soup."

2. TEXT

The TEXT function in Microsoft Excel returns a result converted to text in a given format. The TEXT function is an Excel built-in function that is classified as a Text Function. The TEXT function can be used as part of a formula in a worksheet cell.

Syntax: TEXT (value, format)

Example:

	A	B	C	D	E	F	G
1	7678.868		12-Dec-03		$7,678.87		
2	123.65						
3							
4							
5							
6							

E1 =TEXT(A1, "$#,##0.00")

The following TEXT samples would be returned depending on the Excel spreadsheet above:

= TEXT (A1, "$#,##0.00") = TEXT (A1, "$#,##0.00") = TEXT (A1,"$7,678.87") is the result.

3. TEXTJOIN

The TEXTJOIN function in Microsoft Excel lets you join two or more strings together, with each value separated by a delimiter. The TEXTJOIN function is a Text Function that is included in Excel. The TEXTJOIN function is a worksheet function that can be used in a formula in a worksheet cell.

Syntax:

TEXTJOIN (delimiter, ignore empty, text1, [text2,... text n])

Example:

E2 =TEXTJOIN(",",TRUE,A2,B2,C2,D2)

	A	B	C	D	E	F
1	Text1	Text2	Text3	Text4	Result	
2	A	B	C	D	A,B,C,D	
3	1	2	3	4	1,2,3,4	
4	Tech	On	The	Net	Tech,On,The,Net	
5	alpha	bet			alpha,bet	
6						

The following TEXTJOIN instances would be returned relying on the Excel spreadsheet above:

=TEXTJOIN (",", TRUE,A2,B2,C2,D2) Result is "A,B,C,D"

4. TRIM

The TRIM function in Microsoft Excel returns a text value that has the leading and following spaces removed. It is used to reduce unwanted spaces between words in a string.

The TRIM function is an Excel built-in function that is classified as a Text Function.

Syntax: TRIM (text)

Example:

	A	B	C	D	E
1	Tech on the Net		Tech on the Net		
2	1234				
3	alphabet soup				
4	www.techonthenet.com				
5					

C1 = =TRIM(A1)

=TRIM (A1) Result is "Tech on the Net"

5. LEN

The LEN function in Microsoft Excel returns the length of the provided string. The LEN function is an Excel built-in function that is classified as a String/Text Function. It can be used as a worksheet equation (WS) and a VBA formula (VBA) in Excel.

Syntax: LEN (text)

Example:

	A	B	C	D	E	F
1	Alphabet soup		13			
2	techonthenet.com					
3						
4						
5						
6						

C1 = =LEN(A1)

=LEN (A1) gives 13

6. CLEAN

The CLEAN function in Microsoft Excel eliminates any nonprintable characters from a string. The CLEAN function is an Excel built-in function that is classified as a String/Text Function. The CLEAN function can be used as part of a formula in a worksheet cell.

Syntax: CLEAN (text)

Example:

	A	B	C	D	E	F	G
1	▯hi there		hi there				
2	▯this is a test▯▯						
3							
4							
5							
6							

C1 • fx =CLEAN(A1)

The following CLEAN samples would be returned based on the Excel spreadsheet above:

=CLEAN (A1) Result is "hi there."

7. EXACT

The EXACT function in Microsoft Excel compares different strings and returns TRUE when both values are equal. Otherwise, FALSE will be returned. The EXACT function is an Excel built-in function that is classified as a Text Function.

Syntax: EXACT (text1, text2)

Example:

C1 • fx =EXACT(A1, A2)

	A	B	C	D	E	F	G
1	techonthenet.com		FALSE				
2	Techonthenet.com						
3	alphabet						
4	Alphabet						
5	alphabet						
6							

=EXACT (A1, A2) Result is FALSE

8. PROPER

The PROPER function in Microsoft Excel makes the initial character in each word uppercase and the remainder lowercase. The PROPER function is an Excel built-in function that is classified as a Text Function. The PROPER function can be used as part of a formula in a worksheet cell.

Syntax: PROPER (text)

Example:

	A	B	C	D	E	F
1	alphabet soup		Alphabet Soup			
2	tech on the net					
3	ALPHA BET					
4						
5						
6						

C1 — f_x =PROPER(A1)

=PROPER (A1) Result is "Alphabet Soup."

9. REPLACE

The REPLACE function in Microsoft Excel replaces a string's series of characters with a different set of characters. The REPLACE function is an Excel built-in function that is classified as a String/Text Function. The REPLACE function can be used as part of a formula in a worksheet cell.

Syntax: REPLACE (old text, start, number of chars, new text)

Example:

C1 — f_x =REPLACE(A1, 1, 5, "Beta")

	A	B	C	D	E	F
1	Alphabet soup		Betabet soup			
2	techonthenet.com					
3						
4						
5						
6						

The following REPLACE examples might return based on the Excel worksheet above:

=REPLACE (A1, 1, 5, "Beta") Result is "Betabet Soup."

10. SUBSTITUTE

The SUBSTITUTE function in Microsoft Excel replaces a set of characters with another set. The SUBSTITUTE function is an Excel built-in function that is classified as a Text Function.

Syntax: SUBSTITUTE (text, old text, new text, [nth appearance])

Example:

	A	B	C	D	E	F
1	Alphabet soup		Alphacon soup			
2	techonthenet.com					
3						
4						
5						
6						

C1 fx =SUBSTITUTE(A1, "bet", "con", 1)

The following SUBSTITUTE examples would be returned based on the Excel spreadsheet above:

=SUBSTITUTE (A1, "bet", "con", 1) Result is "Alphacon soup"

11. CONCATENATE

The CONCATENATE function in Microsoft Excel allows you to merge two or more strings. The CONCATENATE function is an Excel pre-defined function that is classified as a Text Function. The CONCATENATE function can be used in a worksheet cell as part of a formula.

Syntax: CONCATENATE (text1, [text2,... text n])

Example:

E2 fx =CONCATENATE(A2,B2,C2,D2)

	A	B	C	D	E
1	Text1	Text2	Text3	Text4	Result
2	E	F	G	H	EFGH
3	5	6	7	8	5678
4	abc	123			abc123
5	TechOnTheNet	.com			TechOnTheNet.com
6					

=CONCATENATE (A2,B2,C2,D2) Result is "EFGH"

12. UPPER

The UPPER function in Microsoft Excel helps to convert text to all uppercase. The UPPER function is part of a Text Function that is included in Excel.

Syntax: UPPER (text)

Example: =UPPER (A1)

Result is "ALPHABET SOUP"

	A	B	C	D	E
1	Alphabet soup		ALPHABET SOUP		
2	TechOnTheNet.com				
3					
4					
5					
6					

Cell C1: =UPPER(A1)

13. LOWER

The LOWER function in Microsoft Excel turns all letters in a string to lowercase. If the string contains any characters that aren't letters, this function does not affect them. The LOWER function is a Text Function that is included in Excel.

Syntax: LOWER (text)

Example:

	A	B	C	D	E
1	Alphabet soup		alphabet soup		
2	TechOnTheNet.com				
3					
4					
5					
6					

Cell C1: =LOWER(A1)

Result: =LOWER (A1)

The result is "alphabet soup"

8.7.3 Logical Functions

Here are some common logical functions:

1. AND

If all conditions are true in Microsoft Excel, the AND function gives TRUE. If any of the conditions are false, it returns FALSE. The AND function is an Excel built-in function that is classified as a Logical Function.

Syntax: AND (condition1, [condition2], ...)

Example:

	A	B	C	D	E	F
1	30			TRUE		
2	www.techonthenet.com					
3						
4						
5						
6						

D1 — fx =AND(A1>10, A1<40)

The following AND samples would be returned based on the Excel spreadsheet above:

A1>10, A1>40) =AND (A1>10, A1>40)

TRUE is the outcome.

2. IF

If the condition is TRUE, the IF function in Microsoft Excel returns one value, and if the condition is FALSE, it gives another value. The IF function is an Excel built-in function that is classified as a Logical Function.

Syntax: IF (condition, value if true, [value if false])

Example:

E2 — fx =IF(B2<10, "Reorder", "")

	A	B	C	D	E	F
1	Item	Quantity		IF Result	IF Result (with ELSE)	
2	Apples	7		Reorder	Reorder	
3	Oranges	30		FALSE		
4	Bananas	21		FALSE		
5	Grapes	3		Reorder	Reorder	
6						

=IF (B2<10, "Reorder", "") "Reorder" is the result.

3. NOT

The NOT function in Microsoft Excel returns the logical value in reverse. The NOT function is an Excel built-in function that is classified as a Logical Function.

Syntax: NOT (logical value)

Example:

	A	B	C	D	E	F
1	5		FALSE			
2	techonthenet.com					
3						
4						
5						
6						

C1 — fx =NOT(A2="techonthenet.com")

=NOT (A2="techonthenet.com") Result is FALSE

4. OR

If the conditions are true, the Microsoft Excel OR function gives TRUE. Otherwise, FALSE is returned. The OR function is an Excel built-in function that is classified as a Logical Function.

Syntax: OR (condition1, [condition2, ... condition_n])

Example:

	A	B	C	D	E	F
1	30		FALSE			
2	techonthenet.com					
3						
4						
5						
6						

C1 — fx =OR(A1<10, A1=40)

=OR (A1=10, A1=40) FALSE is the outcome.

5. SWITCH

The SWITCH equation in Excel compares an expression to a list of values and returns the result. The SWITCH equation is an Excel built-in function that is classified as a Logical Function.

Syntax: SWITCH (expression, value1, result1, value2, result2, ... value_n, result_n [, default])

Example:

=SWITCH (A2,"Excel","TechOnTheNet.com","Minecraft","DigMinecraft.com","Unknown")

Result is DigMinecraft.com

6. TRUE

TRUE is the logical value returned by Microsoft Excel's TRUE function. The TRUE function in Excel is a logical function that comes with the program.

Syntax: TRUE ( )

Example:

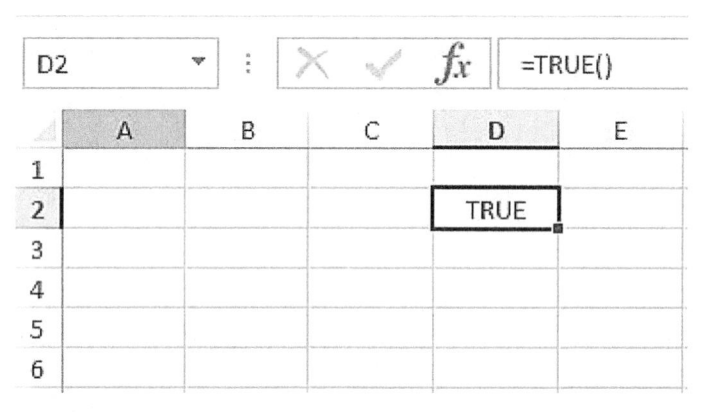

=TRUE () Result is TRUE.

7. FALSE

The FALSE function in Microsoft Excel returns a logical value of FALSE. The FALSE function is an Excel built-in function that is classified as a Logical Function.

Syntax: FALSE ( )

Example:

=FALSE () Result is FALSE

8. IFERROR

If a formula fails, the IFERROR function in Microsoft Excel returns an alternative value. It will look for #N/A, #VALUE!, #REF!, #DIV/0!, #NUM!, #NAME?, or #NULL problems. The IFERROR function is an Excel built-in function that is classified as a Logical Function.

Syntax: IFERROR (formula, alternate_value)

Example:

Column D of the Excel spreadsheet above contains the Price/Unit formula (for example, cell D3 has the formula A3/B3). The formula produces #DIV/0! Errors in cells D3 and D6 because cells B3 and B6 have 0 values. When the formula fails, Column E utilizes the IFERROR function to give 0 as an alternative. Because A3/B3 results in the #DIV/0, the IFERROR function in cell E3 would produce 0 (the alternate value). Error:

=IFERROR (A3/B3,0) 0 is a result

9. IFNA

If a formula returns a #N/A error, the Microsoft Excel IFNA function returns back a substitute value. The IFNA function is an Excel built-in function that is classified as a

Logical Function.

Syntax: IFNA (formula, alternate value)

Example:

When utilizing functions that potentially return the #N/A error, such as VLOOKUP, HLOOKUP, or LOOKUP, the IFNA function comes in handy. The IFNA function can return a different result in some circumstances instead of the #N/A error code.

Column F of the Excel spreadsheet above has a VLOOKUP algorithm for determining the Unit Price for the product name in column E.

When the VLOOKUP function fails, Column G utilizes the IFNA function to return back an alternate value of 0.

Because the VLOOKUP function VLOOKUP (E3,$A$3:$C$7,2, FALSE) resulted in the #N/A error, the IFNA equation in G3 cell would return back a value of 0 (i.e., the alternate value):

	A	B	C	D	E	F	G	H
1						Unit Price		
2	Product	Unit Price	Quantity		Product	Formula Result	IFNA Result	
3	Apples	$14.00	12		Watermelons	#N/A	$0.00	
4	Oranges	$9.80	10		Apples	$14.00	$14.00	
5	Bananas	$34.80	5					
6	Pears	$18.60	9					
7	Grapes	$42.30	40					
8								

=IFNA (VLOOKUP (E3,$A$3:$C$7,2,FALSE),0)

The result is $0.00

10. IFS

The IFS function in Microsoft Excel allows you to define several IF conditions in a single function call. The IFS function is an Excel built-in function that is classified as a Logical Function.

Syntax: IFS (condition1, return1 [,condition2, return2] ... [,condition127, return127])

Example:

	A	B	C	D	E	F
1	Item		IFS Result	IFS Result (with ELSE)		
2	Apple		Fruit	Fruit		
3	Potato		Veg	Veg		
4	Steak		Meat	Meat		
5	Coffee		#N/A	Misc		
6						

C2: =IFS(A2="Apple","Fruit",A2="Potato","Veg",A2="Steak","Meat")

=IFS (A2="Apple","Fruit",A2="Potato","Veg",A2="Steak","Meat")

Result is "Fruit"

8.7.4 Counting Functions

Here are some commonly used counting functions:

1. COUNT

The COUNT function in Microsoft Excel counts the number of cells with numbers and the number of arguments with numbers. The COUNT function is an Excel built-in function that is classified as a Statistical/Counting Function.

Syntax: COUNT (argument1, [argument2, ... argument_n])

Example:

	A	B	C	D	E	F
1	www.techonthenet.com		3			
2		32				
3						
4	123abc					
5		89				
6		-12				

C1: =COUNT(A1:A6)

=COUNT (A1:A6) Result is 3

2. COUNTA

The COUNTA function in Microsoft Excel counts both the number of cells which are not empty and the number of value parameters provided. The COUNTA function is an Excel built-in function that is classified as a Statistical/Counting Function.

Syntax: COUNTA (argument1, [argument2, ... argument_n])

Example:

	A	B	C	D	E	F
1	Last Name	First Name	Math	Biology	Chemistry	
2	Jackson	Joe	A+		B	
3	Smith	Jane		A-	A+	
4	Ferguson	Samantha			C	
5	Reynolds	Allen	B	B		
6	Anderson	Paige	A-			
7	Johnson	Derek			A	
8	**Number of Students**		3	2	4	
9						

Formula in C8: =COUNTA(C2:C7)

=COUNTA (C2:C7) Result is 3 'Number of students with a grade in Math

3. COUNTBLANK

The COUNTBLANK function in Microsoft Excel counts the number of empty cells in a range. The COUNTBLANK function is an Excel built-in function that is classified as a Statistical/Counting Function.

Syntax: COUNTBLANK (range)

Example:

	A	B	C	D	E	F
1	www.techonthenet.com			1		
2	32	89				
3		-12				
4	123abc					
5						
6						

Formula in D1: =COUNTBLANK(A1:A4)

=COUNTBLANK (A1:A4) Result is 1

4. COUNTIF

The COUNTIF function in Microsoft Excel counts the number of cells in a range that fulfills a set of criteria. The COUNTIF function is an Excel built-in function that is classified as a Statistical/Counting Function.

Syntax: COUNTIF (range, criteria)

Example:

F1		fx	=COUNTIF(A2:A7, D2)			

	A	B	C	D	E	F	G
1	Year	Value		Criteria		1	
2	1999	10.5		2000			
3	2000	7.2					
4	2001	200					
5	2002	5.4					
6	2003	8.1					
7	2004	9					
8							

=COUNTIF (A2:A7, D2) Result is 1

5. FREQUENCY

The FREQUENCY function in Microsoft Excel returns the frequency with which values appear in a piece of data. It gives you a vertical array of numbers as a result. The FREQUENCY function is an Excel built-in function that is classified as a Statistical/Counting Function.

Syntax: FREQUENCY (data, intervals)

Example:

A12		fx	=FREQUENCY(B2:B10,D2)	

	A	B	C	D	E	F
1	Name	Test Score		Intervals		
2	Joanne	80		59		
3	Andrew	75		69		
4	George	90		79		
5	Angela	62		89		
6	Marissa	83				
7	John	55				
8	Henry	76				
9	Amanda	93				
10	Darryl	58				
11						
12	2					

=FREQUENCY (B2:B10, D2) Result is 2

6. MIN

The MIN function in Microsoft Excel produces the smallest value from a set of numbers. The MIN function is an Excel built-in function that is classified as a Statistical/Counting Function.

Syntax: MIN (number1, [number2, ... number_n])

Example:

	A	B	C	D	E	F	G
			C2		f_x	=MIN(A2, A3)	
1	Value						
2	10.5		7.2				
3	7.2						
4	200						
5	5.4						
6	8.1						

=MIN (A2, A3) Result is 7.2

7. MAX

The MAX function in Microsoft Excel returns the highest value from a set of numbers. The MAX function is an Excel built-in function that is classified as a Statistical/Counting Function.

Syntax: MAX (number1, [number2, ... number_n])

Example:

	A	B	C	D	E	F	G
			C2		f_x	=MAX(A2, A3)	
1	Value						
2	10.5		10.5				
3	7.2						
4	200						
5	5.4						
6	8.1						

=MAX (A2, A3) Result is 10.5

8. MEDIAN

The MEDIAN function in Microsoft Excel returns the median of the numbers input. The MEDIAN function is an Excel built-in function that is classified as a Statistical/Counting Function.

Syntax: MEDIAN (number1, [number2, ... number_n])

Example:

	A	B	C	D	E	F	G
1	Value						
2	10.5		8.85				
3	7.2						
4	200						
5	5.4						
6	8.1						
7							

C2 → fx =MEDIAN(A2, A3)

=MEDIAN (A2, A3) Result is 8.85

9. MODE

The MODE function in Microsoft Excel delivers the most commonly occurring number in a group of numbers. The MODE function is an Excel built-in function that is classified as a Statistical/Counting Function.

Syntax: MODE (number1, [number2, ... number_n])

Example:

J2 → fx =MODE(B2:H2)

	A	B	C	D	E	F	G	H	I	J	K
1	Course				Grades					MODE Result	
2	Math	78	85	90	72	85	63	97		85	
3	Biology	81	81	81	75	75	75	75		75	
4	Chemistry	80	81	82	83	84	85	86		#N/A	
5											
6											
7											
8											

=MODE (B2:H2) Result is 85

10. GROWTH

The GROWTH function in Microsoft Excel calculates the expected exponential growth based on the input numbers. The GROWTH function is an Excel built-in function that is classified as a Statistical/Counting Function.

Syntax: GROWTH (known_y_values, [known_x_values], [new_x_values], [constant])

Example:

	A	B	C	D	E	F	G
1	X Values	Y Values					
2	3	10.5		7.344380549			
3	4	7.2					
4	120	200					
5	2	5.4					
6	7.5	8.1					
7							

=GROWTH (B2:B6, A2:A6 Result is 7.344380549

8.7.5 Date and Time Functions

Here are some commonly used date and time functions in Excel:

1. DATE

The DATE function in Microsoft Excel gives the serial date value for a date. The DATE function is an Excel built-in function that is classified as a Date/Time Function.

Syntax: DATE (year, month, day)

Example:

	A	B	C	D	E	F	G
1				Result from DATE function			
2	Year	Month	Day	Serial Date	Formatted Date		
3	2016	8	31	42613	8/31/2016		
4	2016	6	30	42551	6/30/2016		
5	2016	1	4	42373	1/4/2016		
6	2016	13	4	42739	1/4/2017		
7							

=DATE (A3,B3,C3)

The result is 42613, "8/31/2016," which is a format that can also be used.

2. DAY

When a date value is given, the Microsoft Excel DAY function will return the day of the month (which is a number between 1 and 31). The DAY function is a Date/Time Function that is included in Excel.

Syntax: DAY (date_value)

Example:

	A	B	C	D	E	F
1	9/1/2012		1			
2	8/31/2012					
3	8/15/2013					
4	8/1/2013					
5						
6						

C1 — fx =DAY(A1)

=DAY (A1) Result is 1

3. EDATE

The EDATE function in Microsoft Excel adds a number of months to a date and provides the result as a serial date. The EDATE function is a Date/Time Function that is included in Excel.

Syntax: EDATE (start_date, months)

Example:

D2 — fx =EDATE(A2,B2)

	A	B	C	D	E
1	Start Date	Months	EDATE Result	Formatted Result	
2	Jan 26, 2016	1	42426	Feb 26, 2016	
3	Feb 15, 2016	2	42475	Apr 15, 2016	
4	Mar 4, 2016	6	42617	Sep 4, 2016	
5	Jun 30, 2016	-1	42520	May 30, 2016	
6					

The EDATE function returns a serial date, which can be seen in column C above. Rather than a serial date, you'll usually want a formatted date. The serial date returned by the EDATE function, formatted with mmm d, yyyy, is shown in Column D.

=EDATE (A2,B2) Result is 42426 ', which can be formatted as "Feb 26, 2016"

4. EOMONTH

When a specified number of months to date are added, the Microsoft Excel EOMONTH function calculates the last day of the month. A serial date is returned as a result. The EOMONTH function is a Date/Time Function that is included in Excel.

Syntax: EOMONTH (start_date, months)

Example:

	A	B	C	D
1	Start Date	Months	EOMONTH Result	Formatted Result
2	Jan 26, 2016	0	42400	Jan 31, 2016
3	Feb 15, 2016	1	42460	Mar 31, 2016
4	Apr 1, 2016	2	42551	Jun 30, 2016
5	Feb 15, 2016	-2	42369	Dec 31, 2015

Formula in D2: =EOMONTH(A2,B2)

The EOMONTH function returns a serial date, which can be seen in column C above. Rather than a serial date, you'll usually want a formatted date. The serial date returned by the EOMONTH function, formatted with mmm d, yyyy, is shown in Column D.

The result of =EOMONTH (A2,B2) is 42400 "Jan 31, 2016" is a format that can also be used.

5. HOUR

The HOUR function in Microsoft Excel returns the hours (a number between 0 and 23) from a time value. The HOUR function is a Date/Time Function that is included in Excel.

Syntax: Hour (serial_number)

Example:

	A	B	C	D
1	8/10/2012 1:07 PM		13	
2	38011.3			

Formula in C1: =HOUR(A1)

=HOUR (A1) Result is 13

6. MINUTE

The MINUTE function in Microsoft Excel returns the minutes (a number between 0 and 59) from a time value. The MINUTE function is a Date/Time Function that is included in Excel.

Syntax: MINUTE (serial_number)

Example:

	A	B	C	D
1	Date Value	Result		
2	Mar 31, 2016 2:10 PM	10		
3	Apr 1, 2016 5:55 PM	55		
4	8:45 PM	45		
5	0:30	30		
6				

B2 =MINUTE(A2)

=MINUTE (A2) Result is 10

7. TIME

Given an hour, minute, and second value, the Microsoft Excel TIME function outputs a decimal number between 0 and 0.999988426. A result of 0 corresponds to 12:00:00 AM, whereas 0.999988426 corresponds to 11:59:59 PM. The TIME function is a Date/Time Function that is included in Excel.

Syntax: TIME (hour, minute, second)

Example:

In this example, three columns are added (columns D, E, and F) with distinct forms for the TIME function results:

- The cells in column D have been prepared with a general format so that the decimal result of the TIME function may be seen.
- The default format is h:mm AM/PM in column E because Excel formats the data after entering the formula.
- Cells are formatted in column F with a custom h:mm:ss AM/PM to show the entire hours, minutes, and seconds.

The TIME examples would return the following values based on the Excel spreadsheet:

	A	B	C	D	E	F
1				**Result from TIME function**		
2	Hour	Minute	Second	Decimal Result	Default Format	Full Format
3	0	0	0	0	12:00 AM	12:00:00 AM
4	10	45	8	0.448009259	10:45 AM	10:45:08 AM
5	18	15	30	0.760763889	6:15 PM	6:15:30 PM
6	23	59	59	0.999988426	11:59 PM	11:59:59 PM
7	25	0	0	0.041666667	1:00 AM	1:00:00 AM
8	1	120	0	0.125	3:00 AM	3:00:00 AM
9	0	0	3600	0.041666667	1:00 AM	1:00:00 AM

=TIME (A3,B3,C3) Result is 0 Represents 12:00:00 AM

8. YEAR

Given a date input, the YEAR function in Microsoft Excel returns a four-digit year (a number between 1900 and 9999). The YEAR function is a Date/Time Function that is included in Excel.

Syntax: YEAR (date_value)

Example:

	A	B	C	D
1	Year	Month	Day	Date
2	1900	4	10	4/10/1900
3	2015	-1	8	11/8/2014
4	2015	0	10	12/10/2014
5	0	10	12	10/12/1900
6	2016	2	0	1/31/2016
7	2015	4	-1	3/30/2015

=YEAR (A1) Result is 1999

9. WORKDAY

The WORKDAY function in Microsoft Excel adds a specified number of workdays to a date and returns a serial date as a result. Weekends are not counted as workdays, and you can exclude holidays from the calculation as well. The WORKDAY function is an Excel built-in function that is classified as a Date/Time Function.

Syntax: WORKDAY (start date, days, [holidays])

Example:

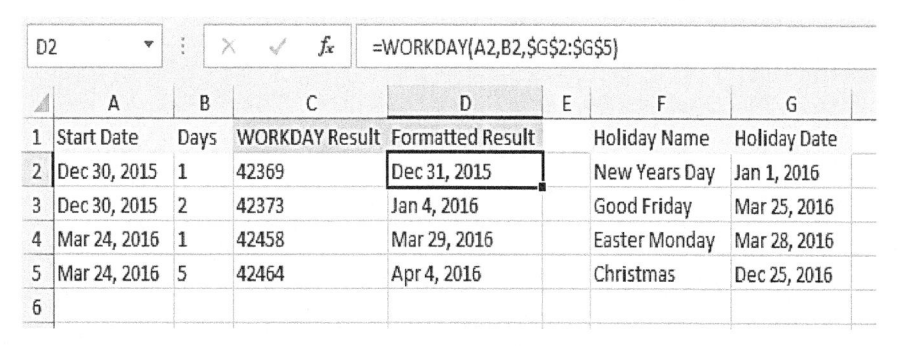

	A	B	C	D	E	F	G
1	Start Date	Days	WORKDAY Result	Formatted Result		Holiday Name	Holiday Date
2	Dec 30, 2015	1	42369	Dec 31, 2015		New Years Day	Jan 1, 2016
3	Dec 30, 2015	2	42373	Jan 4, 2016		Good Friday	Mar 25, 2016
4	Mar 24, 2016	1	42458	Mar 29, 2016		Easter Monday	Mar 28, 2016
5	Mar 24, 2016	5	42464	Apr 4, 2016		Christmas	Dec 25, 2016
6							

=WORKDAY (A2, B2, $G$2:$G$5) Result is 42369

'Which can be formatted as "Dec 31, 2015"WORKDAY (start date, days, [holidays])

8.8 Difference between Formula and Function

Functions, in contrast to formulas, are Excel's pre-built formulas. The 'SUM' function in Excel, for example, makes adding two or more values simple. Use the 'SUM' function instead of constructing your formula to add two numbers. Even though functions are pre-built formulas, they must start with an equal sign. In a formula, you can use more than one function.

DAY #6

"An intelligent mind is an inquiring mind... An intelligent mind is one which is constantly learning"

Bruce Lee

Chapter 9: Working with Excel Tables

9.1 What are Excel Tables?

Tables in Excel are containers for data. Excel tables act as data closets and cabinets, containing and organizing data in spreadsheets. Tables make it simple and fast to examine data in Excel. Excel Tables may help to reduce the amount of time at work. The headers of the excel table will include a reference to that specific column. When dealing with large amounts of data, tables are very useful.

Preparing Data:

Follow these recommendations for data organization before creating the Excel Table.

- ✓ Rows and columns are used to arrange the data, with each row holding information about a single record.
- ✓ Each column in the first row of the list should have a brief, descriptive, and distinct title. Each list column should contain just one kind of data.
- ✓ Each row of the list should include one entry.
- ✓ There should be no blank rows in the list and no empty columns.
- ✓ The data should be separated from the selected data by at least one empty row and one empty column between the list and the other information on the spreadsheet.

9.2 Create an Excel Table

Here are the procedures to convert data into an Excel table once organized, as stated above.

- Select the list of data to include in the table in Excel. These cells may be left blank or filled with data and headers.

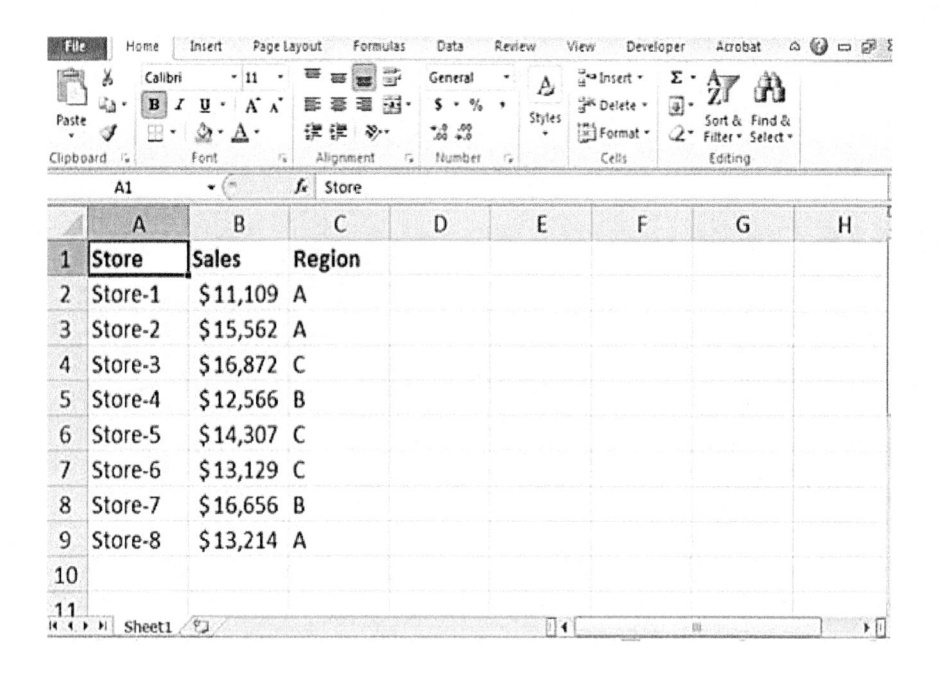

- Select "Table" from the "Insert" menu.

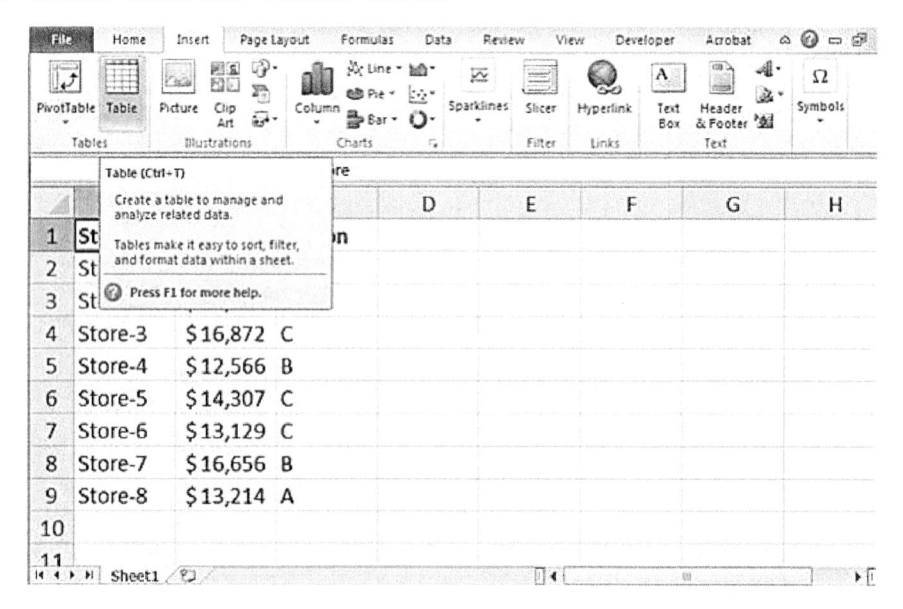

- A rectangular box will display, specifying the data range.

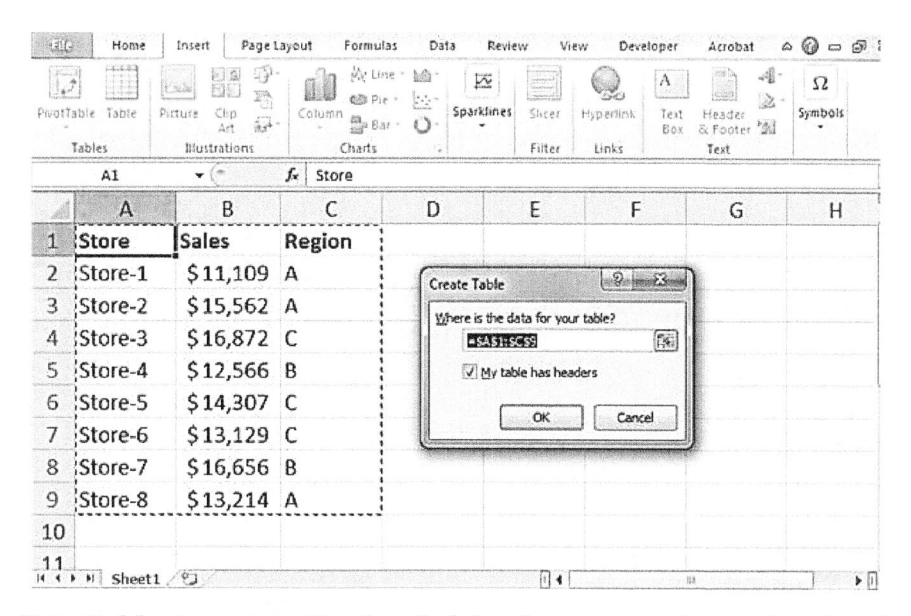

- Select "My Table Contains Headers" if the data range chosen has headers.
- Click "OK".

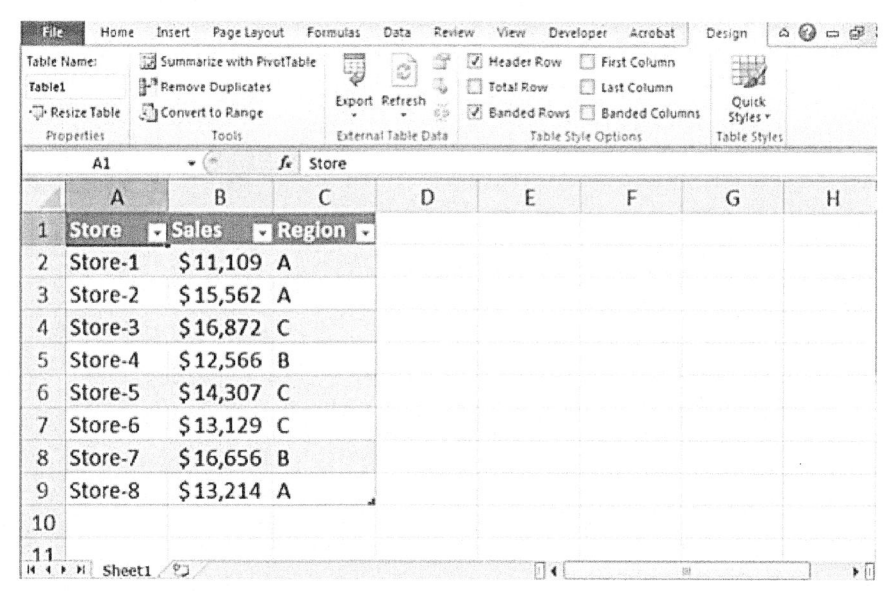

Result. Excel generates a well-formatted table. It may seem to be a standard data range, but numerous sophisticated functions are now available with only a click of a button.

9.3 Why to Use Table

Excel Tables provide several benefits. Tables are mostly used for the following purposes:

Styling and Formatting:

123

After the data has been turned into a table, Excel displays the data into a beautiful table. That may be modified according to requirements. Under the Table Design menu, users may choose from a variety of styles.

Excel Table auto expands when any new data is entered when additional data is added in an adjacent row or column. The table in Excel grows automatically and wraps it. In addition, depending on row and column, the additional rows or columns have the same layout as the remainder of the table.

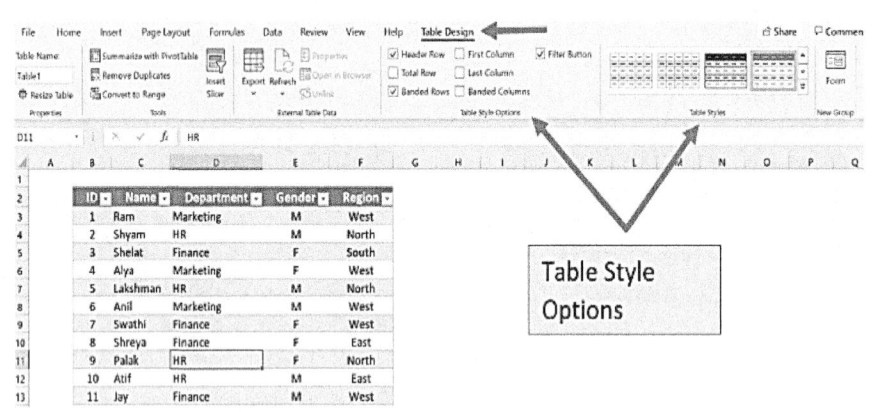

Microsoft excel auto-fill the formula in tables:

The formulae in tables are auto-filled till the final cell. In the first cell in the column, type the formula and then click enter. Until the bottom of the column, Microsoft Excel auto-fill the formula. It improves speed and saves time.

Use of Slicers and Timeline:

Filtering may be done using the slicer in addition to the table's filter choices. It is a really helpful tool for filtering data in an aesthetically compelling manner. The slicer is available underneath the Table Design item in the Tools section. Alternatively, use the Insert tab to add a slicer.

Note: Slicers and a timeline tool have been introduced to Microsoft Excel tables as of Excel 2013.

Edit the table's name:

The ability to name a table is one of the characteristics of Microsoft excel. It makes it simple to refer to the data in the table in formulae. Some names are not acceptable. There are a few guidelines to follow while naming a table:

- Within a worksheet, each table must have its name.
- In a table name, only use letters, numbers, and the underscore character. No spaces or any special characters are allowed.

- A table name must begin with a letter or an underscore; a number cannot be used as the first character.
- A table name may be up to 255 characters long.

The related Table Tools Design tab will show on the ribbon when selecting any cell inside the table. The Table Name is in the Properties section of this tab. Replace the generic name with a new name and then click the Enter key to complete the change.

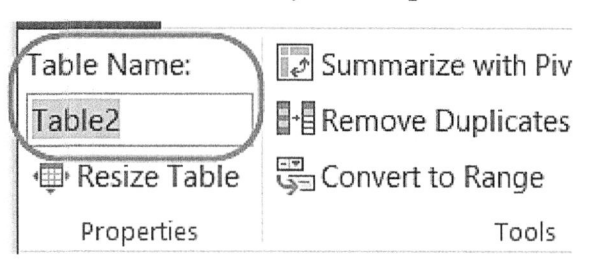

9.4 Excel Tables with Structured Referencing

Another advantage of utilizing Excel Tables is the simplicity of referencing data after generating the table. When referring to data in an Excel Table, there is a particular format to follow:

- It may use names instead of cell references to refer to data.
- To link the data in the two tables. Enter the table's name into Excel, and the option to use that table will appear.
- To get data from a particular column, type the table's full name followed by a square bracket. It will display the column names and relevant choices.

Drag and drop:

Drag and drop data rearrangement is considerably simpler with tables. Drag a table row or column to a new place after selecting it. Excel inserts the selection in the new place without raising an error message about data overwriting.

Totals without the use of formulae:

An optional Total Row is shown in any table. The Total Row may be set to execute operations such as SUM and COUNT without the need to input a formula. These totals will be calculated automatically when the table is filtered to only show visible rows.

Table to create a dynamic chart:

Tables are an excellent method to make dynamic graphs. New data in the table will automatically show on the chart, excluding filtered rows by default.

Tables in Excel are very useful and make working with huge amounts of data a lot simpler. In Excel, tables provide a variety of additional capabilities.

9.5 Pivot Table

What is Pivot Table?

One of the most simple data analysis tools is the pivot table. Many critical business problems can be solved with the help of pivot tables. Pivot Tables are used for a variety of purposes, one of which is to transfer information. The importance of a big, comprehensive data collection may be extracted using a pivot table. Identifying sums, averages, ranges, and outliers are just a few of the data processing tasks a pivot table may do. The table then organizes this data in a straightforward, understandable style that highlights important figures:

1. Add pivot table:

Step two is to pick the data for the table, then go to the Insert Tab on the Excel ribbon, find the tables Group, and select Pivot Table. When the dialogue box appears, double-check that the correct data is chosen, and then choose whether the table should be added as a new worksheet or placed anywhere on the existing worksheet.

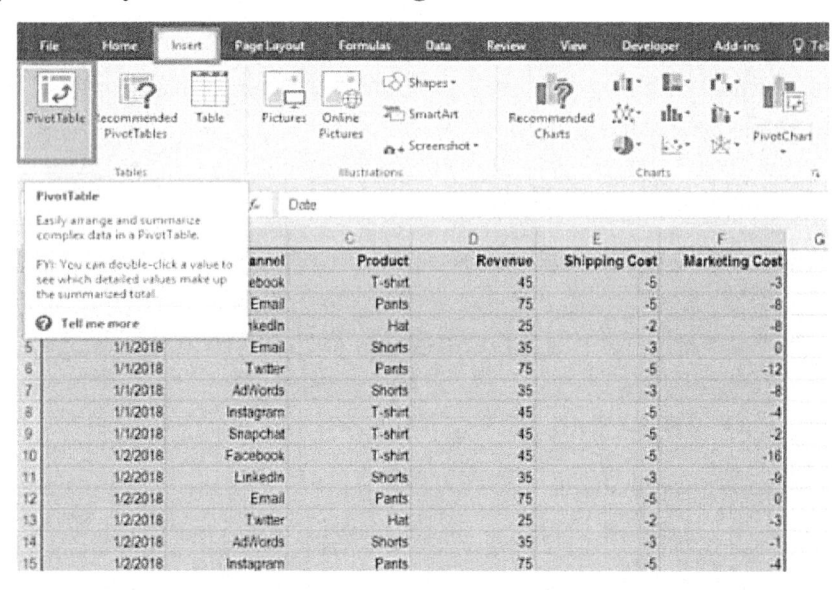

- Create the pivot table's fields:

The "PivotTable Fields" box will display once step two is completed. It is where to drag and drop the displayed choices as accessible fields to customize the fields.

- Sort the data in the table:

Sort the data using different parameters, such as name, value, count, or other criteria, as the basic pivot table is in place. Click the auto-sort option and then "additional sort options" to select various criteria to sort the data. Another alternative is to right-click anywhere around the table and choose Sort, then "additional sort choices" from the menu.

	A	B	C	D	E	F
1	Date	Channel	Product	Revenue	Shipping Cost	Marketing Cost
2	1/1/2018	Facebook	T-shirt	45	-5	-3
3	1/1/2018	Email	Pants	75	-5	-8
4	1/1/2018	LinkedIn	Hat	25	-2	-8
5	1/1/2018	Email	Shorts	35	-3	0
6	1/1/2018	Twitter	Pants	75	-5	-12
7	1/1/2018	AdWords	Shorts	35	-3	-8
8	1/1/2018	Instagram	T-shirt	45	-5	-4
9	1/1/2018	Snapchat	T-shirt	45	-5	-2
10	1/2/2018	Facebook	T-shirt	45	-5	-16
11	1/2/2018	LinkedIn	Shorts	35	-3	-9
12	1/2/2018	Email	Pants	75	-5	0
13	1/2/2018	Twitter	Hat	25	-2	-3
14	1/2/2018	AdWords	Shorts	35	-3	-1
15	1/2/2018	Instagram	Pants	75	-5	-4

- Filter the information:

Adding a filter to the data is a simple method to sort it. With the filter feature, we may see data for particular sub-sections with a single click. An additional box appears at the top of the pivot table, indicating the filter has been applied by dragging the desired category from the list of choices down to the Filters section.

- Modify the data values (calculations):

By default, all data in Excel pivot tables are presented as the total of whatever is displayed in the table. Right-click on the data to alter the value and choose "Value field settings," which will open the box. It is a critical characteristic in accounting and financial analysis since it is often required to switch between units/volume (the count function) and overall cost or income (the sum function).

9.6 Two Dimensional pivot tables

A pivot table with fields on both rows and columns is known as a two-dimensional pivot table.

Follow the steps outlined below to build two-dimensional pivot tables:

- Turn on the Datasheet.
- Select the INSERT tab.
- Select Pivot Chart & Table from the drop-down menu.
- Select all of the information.
- Choose the OK button
- With the pivot table tools, a new sheet will generate.
- Choose the fields you want to work with.

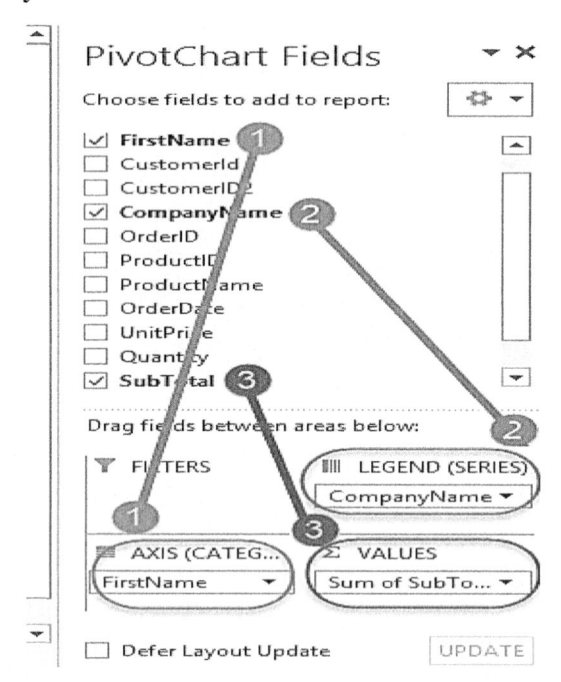

9.7 Uses of Pivot Table

A pivot table allows users to quickly and easily answer business issues.

The following are some examples of pivot table applications:

- In commercial settings, to compute sums or averages.
- To represent totals as a proportion of the total.
- To create a list of distinct values.
- To summarize a complicated report in a 2x2 table.

- To determine a dataset's maximum and lowest values.

9.8 Style and Formatting of Table

Excel spreadsheets may hold a wide range of information, from basic text to complicated calculations. These spreadsheets may grow in complexity and be utilized to make critical choices. It's not only about making Excel spreadsheets vibrant; it's also about utilizing the built-in designs to add meaning. A worksheet user will glance at a column and get what it means despite looking at each formula.

9.9 Excel table styles

Excel tables make it much simpler to examine and manage data by including capabilities like integrated filtering and sorting, calculated columns, structural references, and total rows. On the Design tab, you can alter the standard table format by selecting one of the built-in Table Styles. The Table Layout tab has a variety of style choices.

9.10 Table Style Options

Working with Excel table styles begins with the Design tab. After selecting any cell in a table, it displays in the Table Tools popup tab. The Table Designs gallery has a selection of 50+ built-in styles divided into three categories: light, medium, and dark. A table style in Excel is a formatting template that automatically applies specific styles to table rows and columns, headings, and totals.

The Table Style Options, in addition to table formatting, may be used to design the following table components:

- **Header Row.** The headers continue to appear even when viewing after the data has been structured into a table. Table headers may be shown or hidden using the header row.
- **Banned Row.** When data is turned into an excel table, Excel shades every alternate row by default to make the data easier to read and differentiate. It is referred to as banded rows. Deselect the banded-row choice in the table styles menu under the Table Layout menu to turn this off. A banded column is also an option.
- **Total Row.** Select the Total row option from the Table Design tab in the Table Style settings. Alternatively, choose "table" and then "total row" by right-clicking on any

column in the table. In the end, the total of all the rows in a particular column will be generated. Choose the cell that contains the total; it includes a filter-like option. Choose from a range of functions by clicking that button, such as Minimum, Maximum, Summation, and so on.

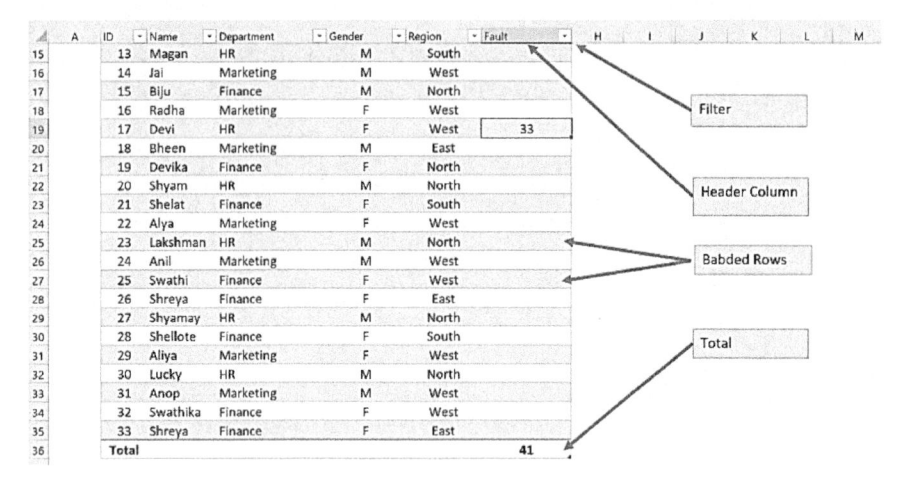

9.11 Select Table Style When Creating a Table

To make a table with a particular style, follow these steps:

1. Choose the cell to create a table.
2. Format Table may be found under the Styles category on the Home page.
3. To apply a style, go to the Table Styles collection and click it.

9.12 Change the table style

Follow these procedures to change the style of an existing table:

1. To change the style of a cell in the table, click it.
2. Click the More button on the Design tab in the Table Styles category to see all possible Excel Table styles.
3. When you click on the style you want to use, Excel will display you a preview.

Click on the new style to apply it.

Note: Right-click on a style and choose Apply and Clear Formatting to apply a new style and erase any current formatting.

9.13 Remove table formatting

Clear the table style in this manner to retain all of the functionality of an Excel table while removing just the formatting, such as banded rows, shading, and borders:

1. Select any cell from the row or column in the table.
2. Click the More button in the Table layout category on the Design tab.
3. Click clear beneath the table style templates.
4. All formatting of table will remove.

DAY #7

"There is no beginning, there is no end. There is only becoming."

Selene

Chapter 10: Creating Charts

Excel is used to store data by businesses of various sizes and in a variety of sectors. Excel can assist you in converting your spreadsheet data into charts and graphs so you can get a clear picture of your data and make informed business choices.

10.1 What are Excel Charts?

A chart is a visual demonstration of data in both columns and rows in a visual format. Charts are often used to analyze data sets for trends and patterns. Charts and graphs help you make sense of your data by visualizing quantities in an easy-to-understand way. Even though the words are often used simultaneously, they are distinct. Graphs are the simplest basic visual representation of data, and they usually show data point values across time.

Charts are more complicated because they enable you to compare parts of a data set to other data in the same set. Charts are also seen to be more visually appealing. In presentations, charts and graphs are often used to provide a rapid overview of progress or outcomes to management, clients, or team members. You can make a chart representing almost any statistical data, saving your time and effort to sifting through spreadsheets to discover connections and trends.

Excel makes it simple to construct charts and graphs, particularly because you can keep your data in an Excel Workbook rather than importing it from another software. Excel also comes with several pre-made charts of different kinds from which you may choose the one that best reflects the data connections you wish to emphasize.

10.2 Types of Charts

Excel has a vast chart collection to help you graphically display your data. While many chart styles may be appropriate for a particular data set, choosing the best match for your data is critical. You may, of course, add graphical components to a chart or graph to improve and personalize it. Excel 2013 and later versions include a feature that evaluates your data and recommends the chart style you should use.

The most frequently used Excel charts and when you should use them are shown below:
- Column Charts.
- Bar Charts.

- Pie Charts.
- Scatter Charts.
- Line Charts.
- Combo Charts.

The kind of data you wish to analyze and report determines the type of excel charts you use for analysis and interpretation and what you want to do with it. Make data visual.

- Sort and classify information.
- Discover a link between the data.
- Recognize the data's structure.
- Recognize how data is distributed.
- Recognize the overlap of data.
- Look for patterns and trends.
- Identify outliers and other data abnormalities.
- Make predictions about future trends.

Hereafter, you will understand the right chart type to use.

<u>Column Charts:</u>

Column charts are ideal for comparing data or if you have several categories of one variable. Clustered, stacked, 100 percent stacked, 3-D clustered, 3-D stacked, 3-D % stacked, and 3-D 100 pictured stacked are the seven-column chart styles available in Excel. In this graph, the values flow vertically.

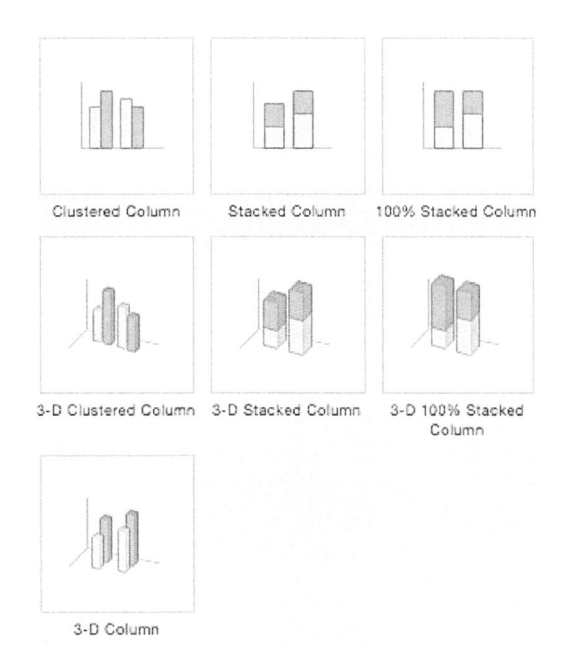

You may compare data from similar categories using column charts and see how variables' independence evolves. Compare the contributions of various class members, and contrast negative and positive values.

Bar Charts:

The primary difference between a bar chart and a column chart is that the bars in a bar chart are horizontal rather than vertical. Although bar charts and column charts are used frequently, some prefer column charts when dealing with negative values since it's simpler to perceive negatives vertically on a y-axis.

You may use a bar chart when the axis labels are too lengthy to fit in a column chart.

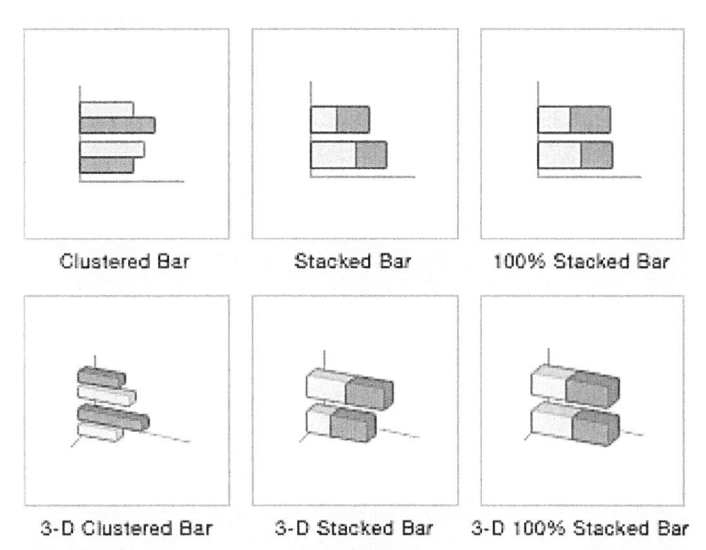

Pie Charts:

To compare percentages of a whole (the sum of the values in your data), use pie charts. Each value is represented as a pie slice, allowing you to see the proportions. There are five pie charts: pie, pie of pie (which divides one pie into two to illustrate sub-category proportions), the pie bar, 3-D pie, and a doughnut.

When you wish to display a 100% data composition, use a pie chart. Put another way, only use a pie chart to illustrate the data composition when you only have one set of data and fewer than five categories to plot. In general, pie charts depict the part-to-whole connection in your data. When your data is expressed as a percentage, a pie chart is an ideal option for you. Only use a pie chart to display data composition when the pie pieces are all the same size.

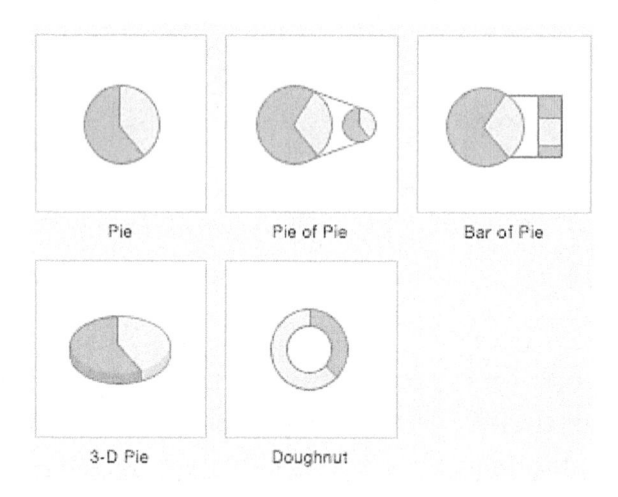

Scatter Charts:

Scatter charts are used to illustrate how one variable influences another. They are similar to line graphs in that they help demonstrate variation in variables over time. It is referred to as correlation. Bubble charts, which are a common chart form, are classified as scatter. Scatter, scatter with lines and markers, scatter with smooth lines, scatter with straight lines and markers, scatter with straight lines, bubble, and 3-D bubble are the seven scatter chart choices.

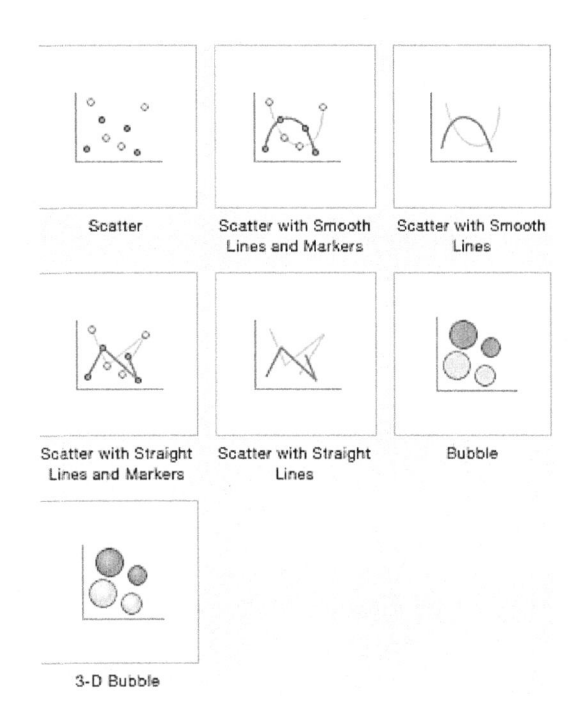

You should consider a scatter chart when analyzing and reporting the correlation between two variables.

Line Charts:

Instead of static data points, a line chart is best for displaying patterns over time. The lines link each data point, allowing you to observe how the value(s) grew or dropped over time. Line, stacked line, 100% stacked line, line with markers, stacked line with markers, 100% stacked line with markers, and 3-D line are the seven-line chart choices.

Line charts are used to show/focus on data patterns, particularly long-term trends between data values. Another scenario you may use a line chart is when you have a lot of data points to display, and a column or bar chart would be too

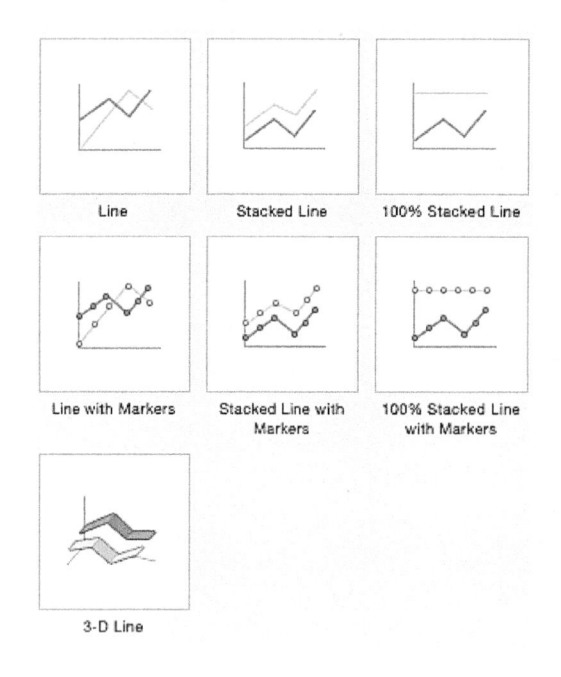

Combo Charts:

A Combo Chart is a mixture of two separate chart kinds, such as a column chart and a line chart. Multiple chart types are shown in a single Combo Chart. Combo charts are capable of plotting data of varying sizes. Can demonstrate how one thing influences another.

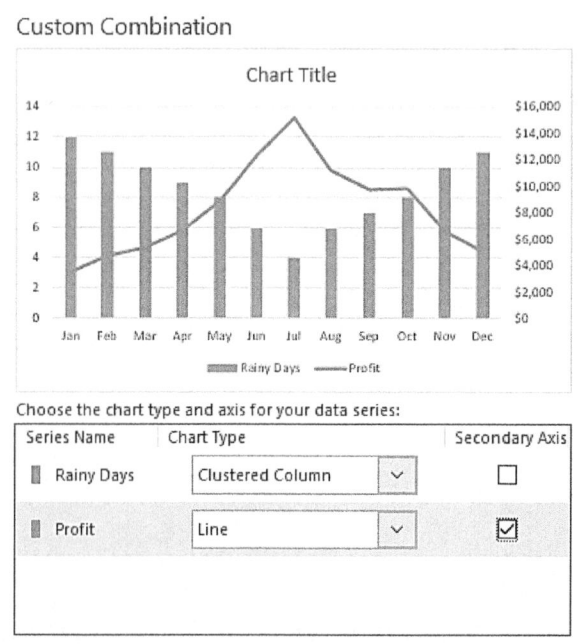

There are additional four minor chart categories. These charts are more case-specific:

- Area Charts.
- Stock Charts.
- Surface Charts.
- Radar Charts.

Area Charts:

Area charts, like line charts, depict variations in values over time. On the other hand, region charts help highlight variations in change among several variables since the area under each line is solid.

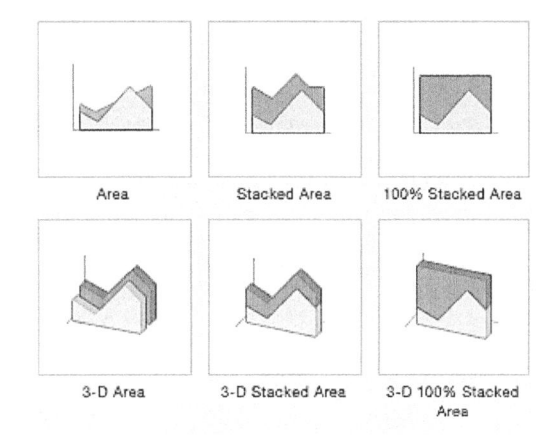

Stock Charts:

This kind of chart is used in financial research. However, if you wish to show the range of a number and its precise value, you may utilize those charts in any situation. Choose from stock chart choices such as high-low-close, open-high-low-close, volume-high-low-close, and volume-open-high-low-close.

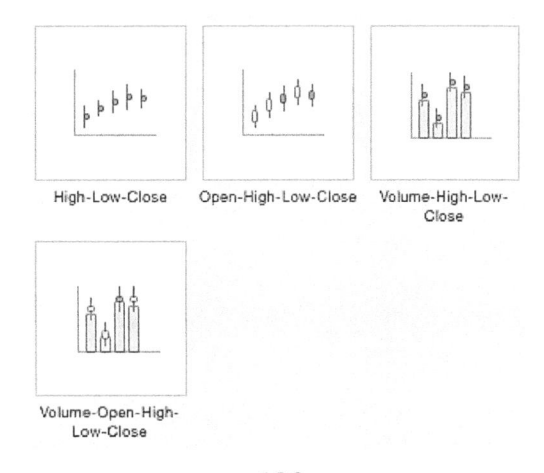

Surface Charts:

To depict data in a 3-D environment, use a surface chart. Large data sets with more than two factors and data sets with categories inside a single variable benefit from this extra plane. Surface charts, on the other hand, can be tough to read, so be sure your audience knows what they're looking at. 3-D area, wireframe 3-D surface, contour, and wireframe contour are the options available.

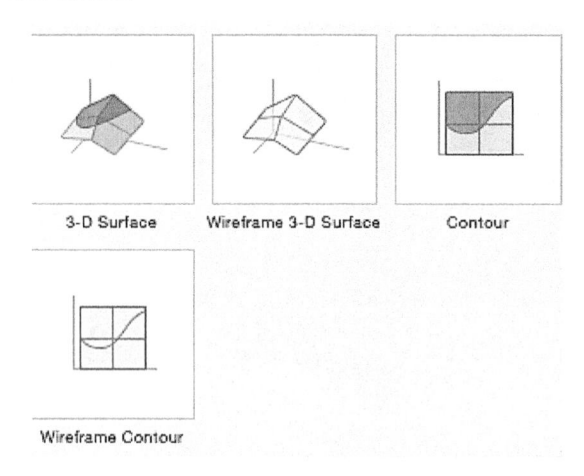

Radar Charts:

A radar chart is useful for displaying data from many variables that are related to one another. The central point is the starting point for all variables. The key to using radar charts is to compare all individual factors concerning one another; they're often used to compare the strengths and weaknesses of individual goods or workers. Radar, radar with markings, and filled radar are the three kinds of radar charts.

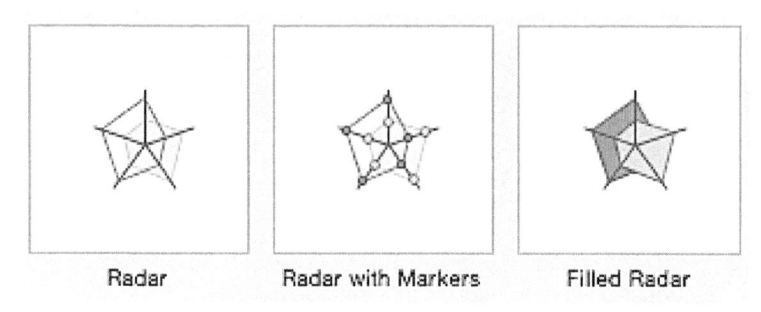

10.3 Creating Chart in Excel

Charts are a wonderful method to visually communicate facts and information. The data that charts depict is their basis. The first and most significant step in producing a chart is selecting the appropriate data. You must first enter your data into Excel. By moving your mouse across the cells containing the data you wish to utilize in your graph, you can highlight them. You may now choose your chart type to display your data after entering your data and selecting the cell range.

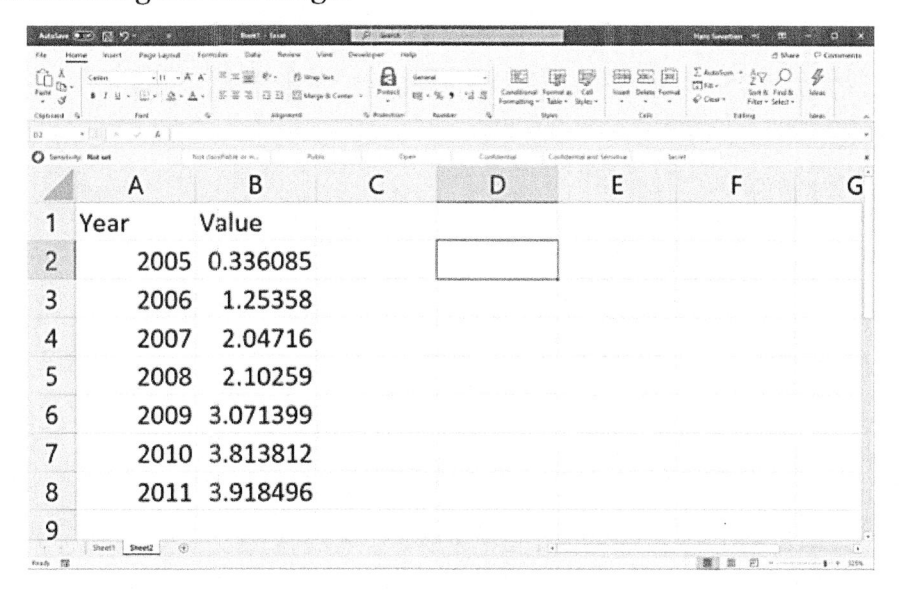

For example, suppose you have a spreadsheet with two data columns. The variable Year is in column A, while the variable Value is in column B. You wish to make a chart with the variable value on the vertical axis and the year on the horizontal axis.

After choosing your data for the chart, insert a chart into your spreadsheet using the instructions below:

1. Choose the information you want to use.
2. On the ribbon, select the Insert tab.

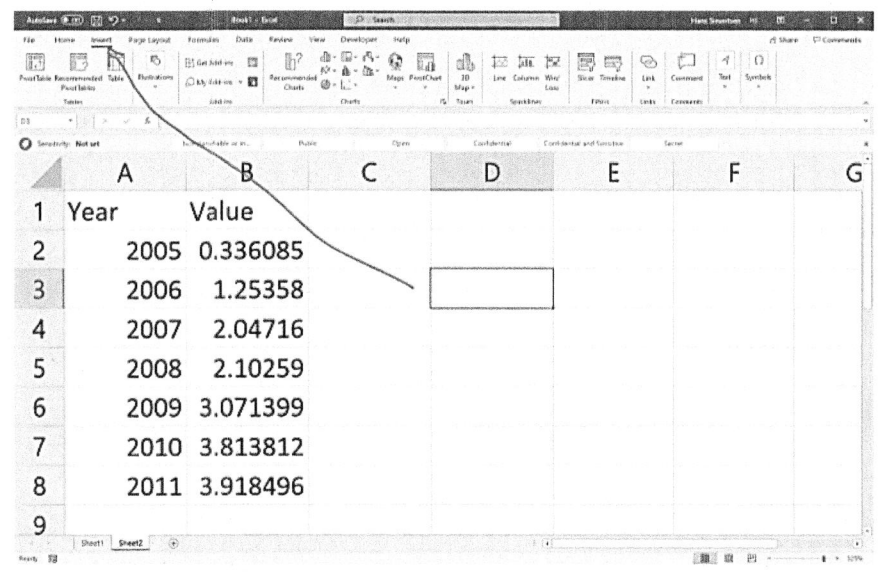

3. On the ribbon, select Insert Chart.

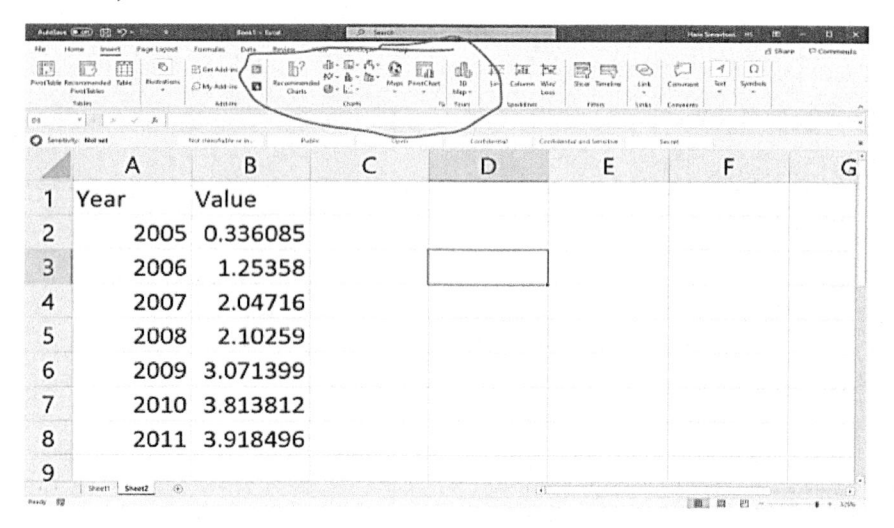

4. To see the previews, navigate through the Chart settings.

5. Please insert the desired chart by clicking on it. In the figure below line chart is used.

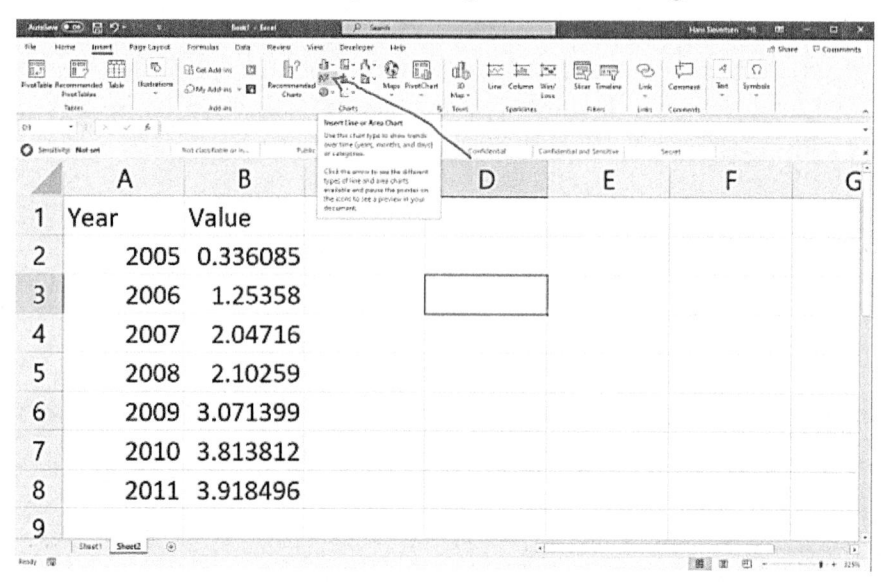

6. When you click the line chart icon, a menu with several chart types appears.

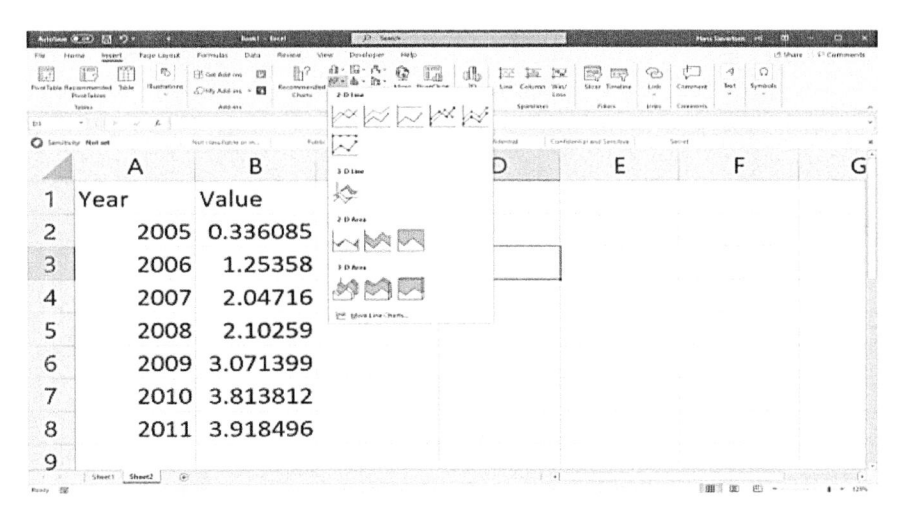

7. To create the chart, you must first tell Excel what data to use. After selecting the chart canvas (by just clicking on it), go to the "Chart Design" tab and choose "Select Data" (see below). An alternative way is you can also right-click on the graph and select "Select Data."

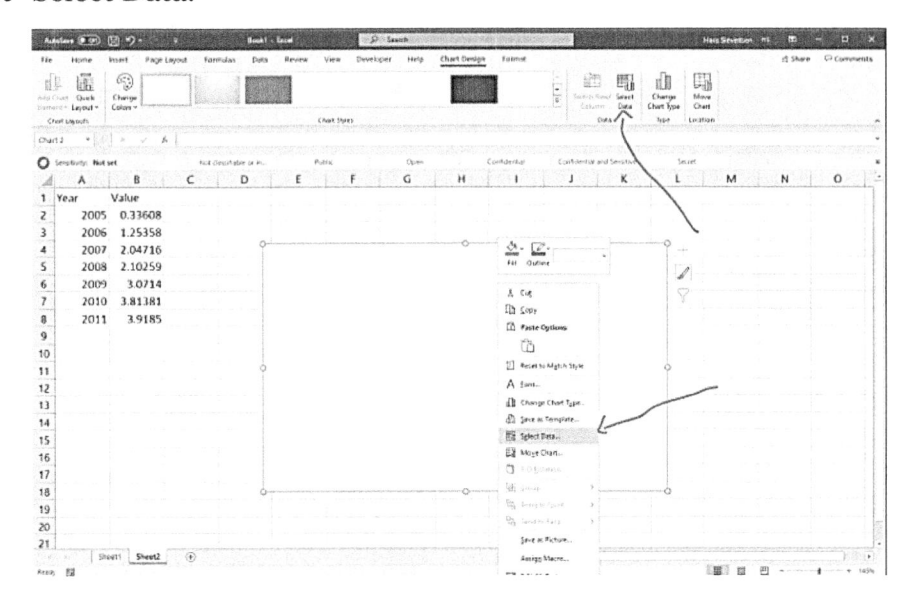

8. The menu below shows how to pick data. You may pick the whole data region to be used at the top. You may choose which data to display on the left panel's vertical axis (y-axis) and which variable to display on the right panel's horizontal axis (x-axis).

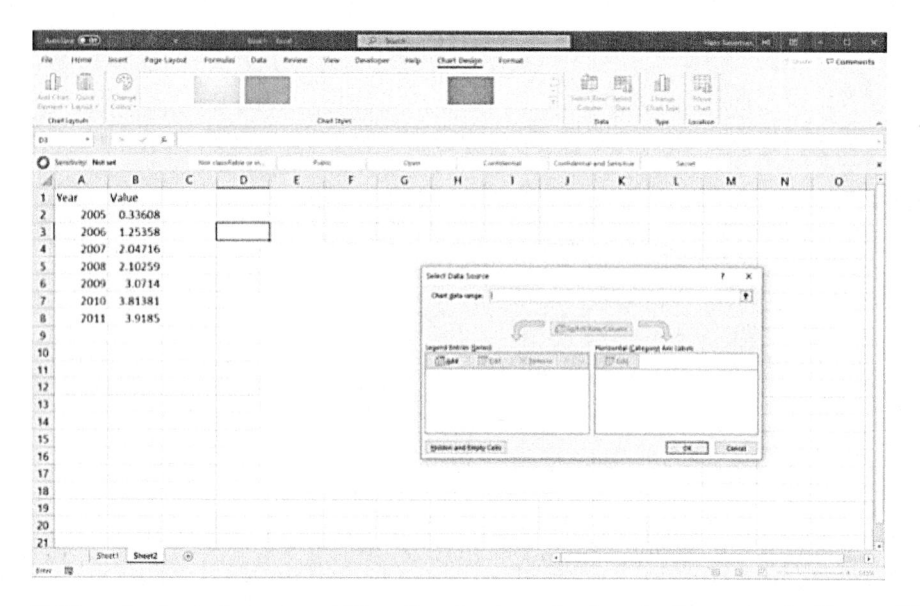

9. Let's tell Excel what data to utilize for the vertical axis first. As indicated below, click "Add."

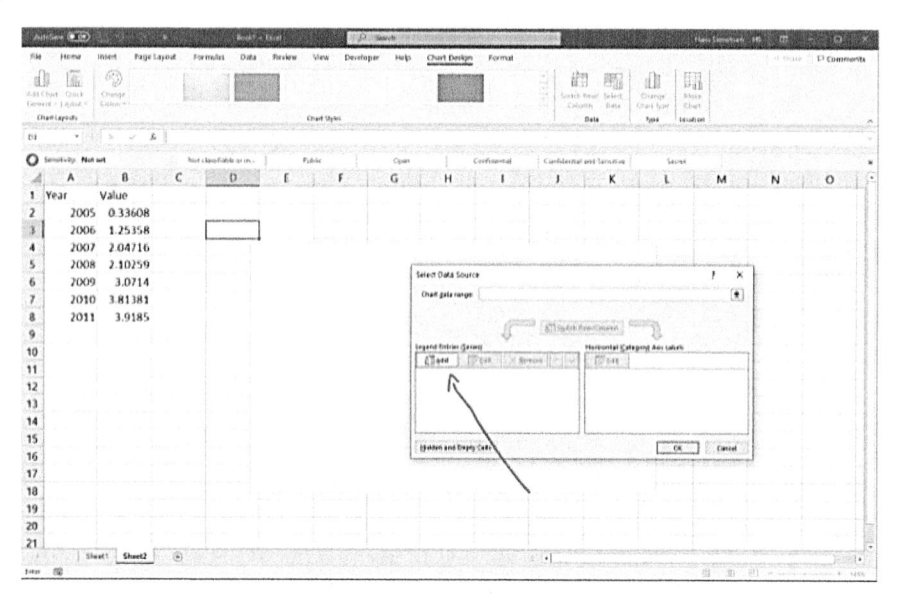

10. A menu should now display, identical to the one below. You may give the series a name and describe its content here. You may manually type the description of the sequence in the "Series name" field.

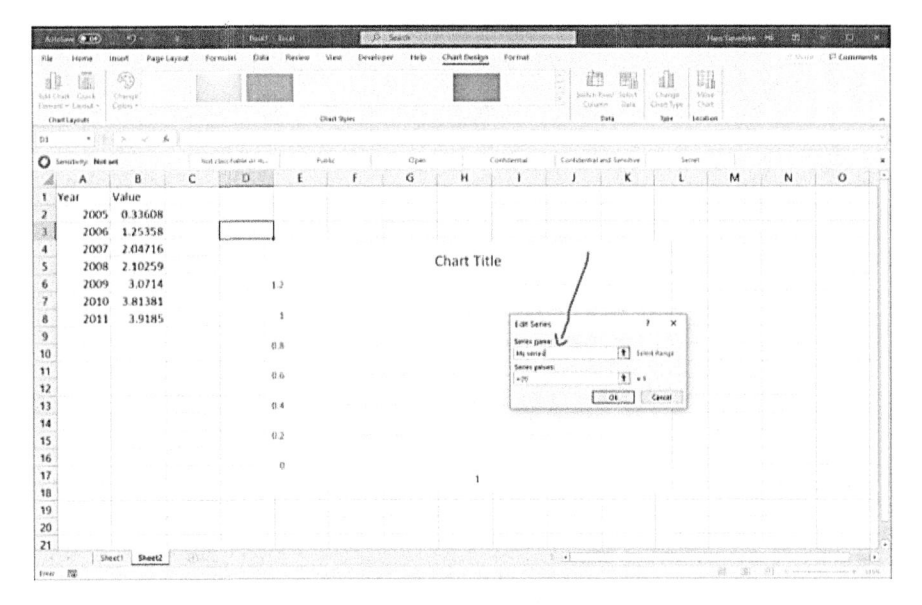

11. For the "Series Values," click the arrow up icon. Select all of the cells containing the values you want to display on the vertical axis.

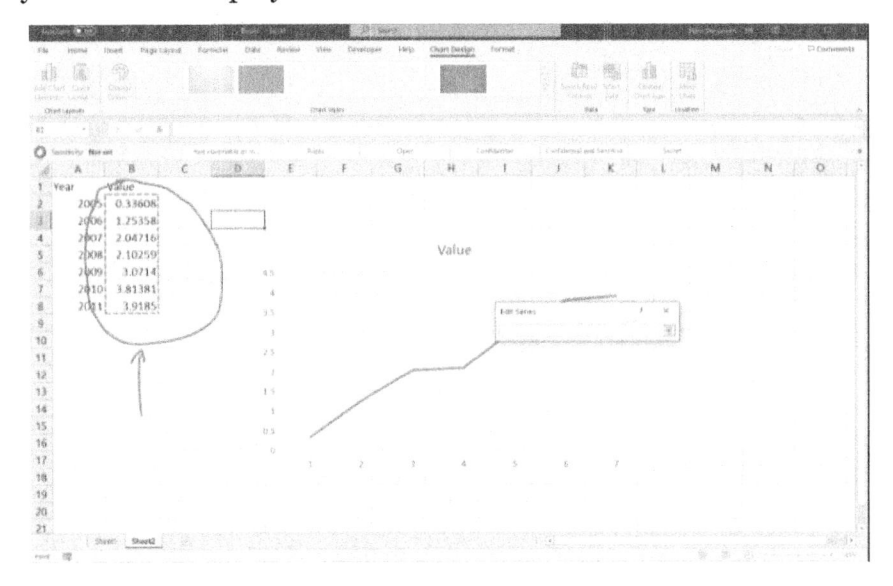

12. To pick the series for the horizontal axis, go to the right panel and click "Edit." Select the data for the horizontal axis using the same technique as for the vertical axis and click OK.

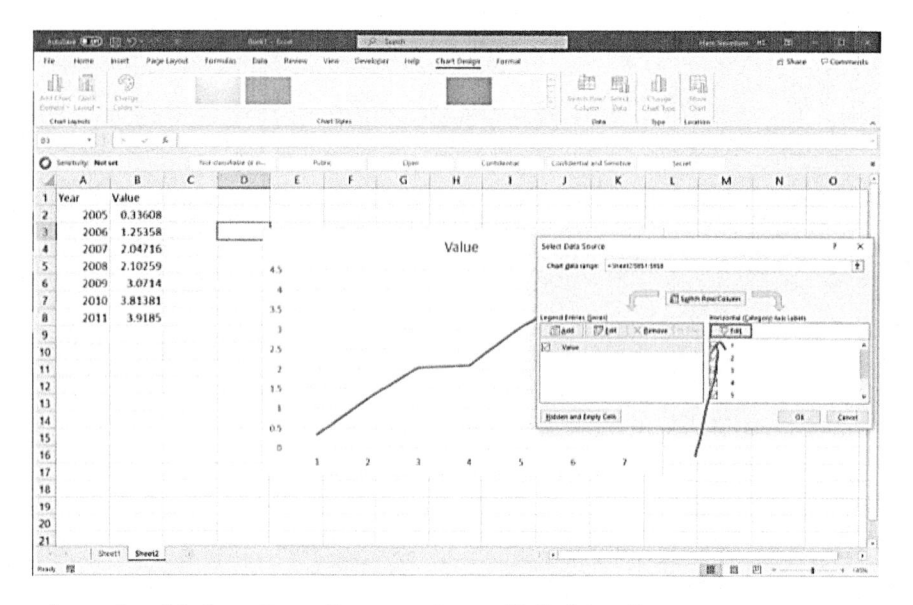

13. To complete the "Select Data" operation, click "OK."

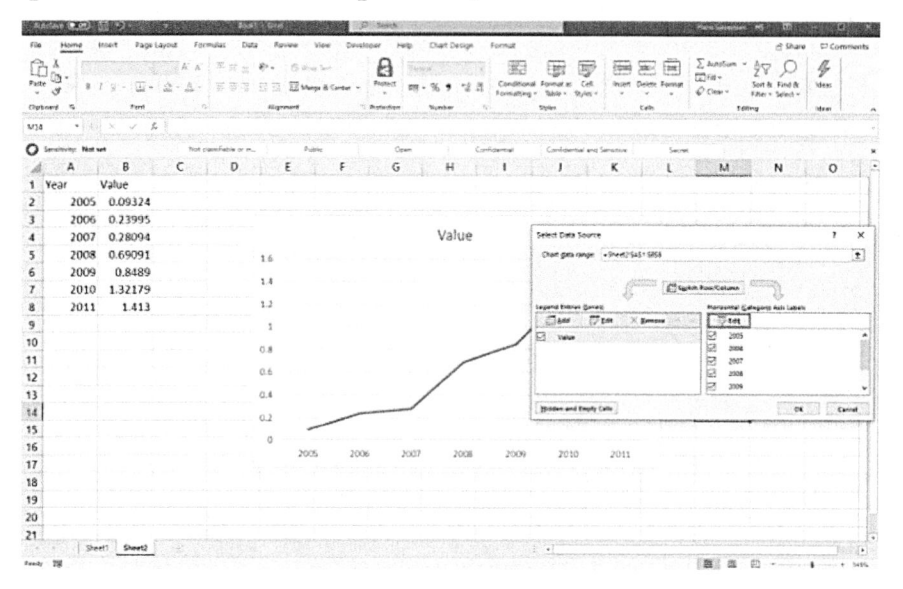

14. Your Chart will be inserted in your worksheet.

146

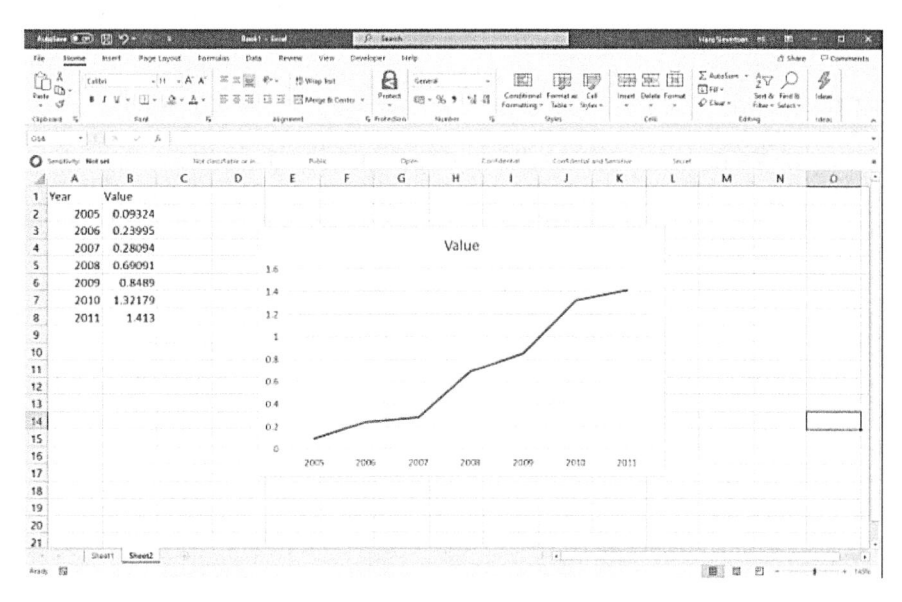

To make any chart, follow the procedures shown above. The technique for selecting data stays the same.

How to modify Excel Charts

Once the chart is in Excel, you may change its appearance and location in various ways. A few options are shown below:

- To add any labels (such as the title or axis), click Add Chart Element in the Chart Layouts group on the Design ribbon and choose the desired label.
- Use the Chart Tools Design ribbon to alter the chart type, data, or location.
- You can choose the Format Selection icon in the Current Selection group from the Chart Tools Format ribbon after selecting an element on the chart. You can adjust the shape, style, and color of the text using the Formatting Task window.

10.4 How to Create a Process- Behavior Chart in Excel

The process-behavior chart, also known as a control chart, is frequently used to identify if a manufacturing or business process is statistically controlled. The processes for making a control chart in Excel are outlined below.

1. Arrange Data:

Of course, the first step is to enter the data you've gathered into the spreadsheet. Fill in the blanks with your data in rows, one for each sample. In the sample's row, each sample observation will be recorded as a separate cell. It would be perfect if you could additionally take advantage of headings to assist you in maintaining track of what's what.

2. Calculate Sample Statistics:

You will compute sample statistics for each control chart, including the average and range of the data plotted on the control chart. These statistics should be calculated using conventional Excel formulas on the same row as the relevant sample. The data's average is determined with the average function, while the range is derived with the maximum and minimum functions.

3. Calculate Center Line and Control Limits

The next step is to calculate the control chart's major components. The upper control limit (UCL) and lower control limit (LCL) are two control limits. To determine these limitations, you must first determine the Centerline. The average or media of your data is equal to the Center Line. Upper control limits are always set three standard deviations above the mean value, while lower control limits are set below.

10.5 Creating Process- Behavior Chart

Following, are the steps to construct a control chart after you've selected all of the necessary data:

- Navigate to the Insert tab to create a Line Chart.
- Click on the Charts tab on the ribbon.
- Select the desired chart from the Insert Line chart selection list.
- Select the OK option.
- Your spreadsheet will add with the chart.

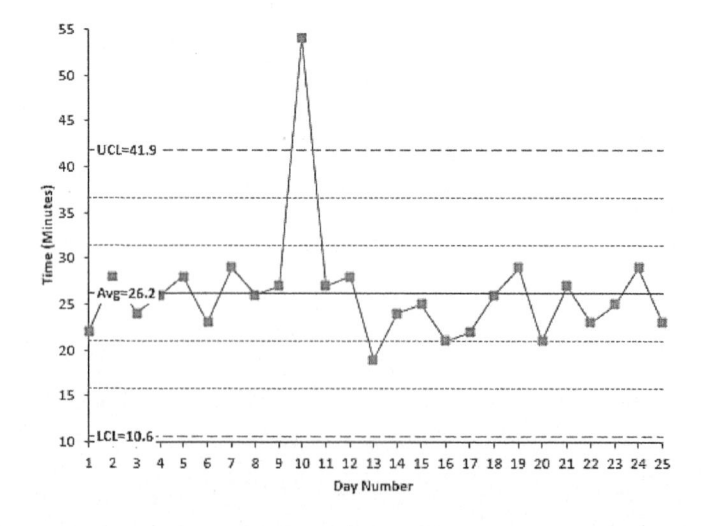

Chapter 11: Magical Tips for Excel

Microsoft Excel is a vital software program for every company. Some individuals like Excel's features, believing it to be a valuable tool for managing, reporting and illustrating data tables. Excel hints can make your life simpler and more effective while working with this multi-tool database. Almost every office task is completed with the assistance of magical software. It may seem at first glance to be software with just tables and slots for data entry.

However, this description falls well short of the program's true capabilities. You need to know how to use Excel to manage anything from your workplace finances to the data needed to run a nation.

Here are a few useful Excel tips and techniques to help you enhance your Excel skills.

11.1 Paste Special

Copy and paste are one of Excel's most basic and often used operations. However, we often transfer over an unwanted format or duplicate a formula when we only want a value. You may choose which components of the copied cell to carry across using Paste Special. **Ctrl+Alt+V** to bring up Paste Special and make your choice once you've copied your cell.

11.2 How to add multiple rows

Between existing rows, we often need to add new rows. Ctrl+ shift+ is a useful shortcut, particularly since you can toggle the + to add several rows. When adding in bulk, it's often faster to highlight the number of rows you want to enter and then right-click than click on the insert option. It will add the number of rows you have highlighted.

11.3 Conditional Formatting

When analyzing data sets, conditional formatting is a great visual aid. It changes the color of a cell depending on the data within and the criteria you provide. It is used to make heat maps, color label common data, and a lot more. Let's have a look at how you may start using this functionality in your spreadsheets:

- Make a selection of the cells you wish to work with.
- From the Ribbon, choose the Home tab, then Conditional Formatting.

- From the drop-down menu, choose the reasoning you wish to employ.
- A pop-up window will open where you can give Excel the rules it needs to correctly sort your data. When you're finished, click OK to view your findings.

11.4 How to detect duplicate data

Follow the instructions below to identify and highlight repeating groups in Excel:

- Choose a range of cells to work with. You must choose whatever data you wish to work with, just as you do with any other Excel function.
- Navigate to the Styles section of the Home tab. To open a drop-down menu, click Conditional Formatting.
- Choose the Duplicate values option under Highlight Cell Rules.
- You will now see a menu appear. It is where you may choose how you want your duplicate cells to be formatted.
- To detect the duplicates, click OK.

11.5 Use Shortcut Keys

Excel is very comprehensive, which means many tools are used inside it, and therefore numerous skills may be practiced and honed.

Knowing the major Excel keyboard shortcuts can help you be more productive, quicker, and more effective while creating financial models or conducting financial analysis.

In the Appendix at the end of this book you can find the 50 most useful shortcuts.

11.6 Copy-Paste Formulas without Changing References

It occurs regularly. When you attempt to duplicate a formula-filled cell to another cell, everything gets jumbled up. It occurs because when you copy to a different place, the references change.

To use this trick, follow the step written below:

- Make a selection of the cells you wish to duplicate.

- Go to the Home page and choose Number. Select Text from the Number format drop-down menu. The cell's format will change to Text.
- To enter the edit mode, press F2. Now press Enter while holding down the Control key.
- Make a copy of the cells.
- Paste into the desired cell.
- Change the format to General from Text.
- F2 is pressed, then Control + Enter is pressed.

11.7 Debugging Formula

A comma was missing, the reference was incorrect, the argument was missing, the parentheses were wrong, etc. There might be hundreds of causes for a formula's incorrect outcome.

It might not be easy to debug a formula, mainly if it was designed by someone else. Here's the trick how to make things straightforward. To troubleshoot a formula, do the following:

- Choose the cell with the formula.
- Click to Formulas.
- Select Formula Auditing from the drop-down menu.
- Select Formula Evaluation from the menu.
- To show the stages in which Excel evaluates the calculation, click Evaluate.

11.8 Need to Delete All Comments

When you start again, one of the spreadsheet procedures you do is erase all of the comments. Here's an easy method to select all of the comments and remove them all at once:

All of the cells are selected.

- Click Home –> Editing –> Find and Select –> Special.
- In the Go to Special Dialogue box, choose Comments.
- Click the OK button.

It will pick all of the cells in which there are comments. Now right-click any of the chosen cells and choose Delete Comment.

11.9 Custom Sorting

Many of the most often utilized functions in Excel is sorting. Sorting alphabetically, by value (most significant to smallest or smallest to largest), by the weekday (Mon, Tue, Wed,.....), or by monthly names are all typical examples (Jan, Feb..)

While these are built-in sorting criteria, you may add additional ones based on your data. Here are the steps to use this trick:

- Select File –> Options from the File menu.
- Select Advanced from the list in the main window of the Excel Options Dialogue Box. Scroll down and choose Edit Custom List from the advanced menu.
- In the Custom Lists dialogue box, in the List Entries box, write your criteria. Separate your criteria with a comma.
- Select Add and Click Ok.

To sort your Data through custom criteria, you need to follow these steps:

- Select the data set.
- Go to Data –> Sort.
- In the Order drop-down list, select Custom List.
- Select the criteria and click OK.

11.10 Bullets in Excel

If you have a list in the same cell, this could be THE lifesaver trick for you. Use this tip to insert bullets to make your list look good.

Following are the steps to use this trick:

- Go to the cell and double click to get into edit mode
- Press Alt + 7 or Alt + 9

11.11 Multi-Level Sorting

Multi-level sorting allows you to sort one column, then the next while keeping the first column sorted.

Following the steps to perform this trick:

- Choose the whole collection of data.
- Select Sort and Filter from the Data menu.
- Click Sort
- Select Column Sort by, Sort On, and Order values from the drop downs in the Sort dialogue box [for the subject column, i.e., the first level sorting].
- At the top, choose the Add Level option. It will add another level of sorting.
- Select the sort criteria once more.

11.12 Scrollable List in Excel

When you have extensive data collection and don't want to pick the whole screen, you'll need a scrollable list.

- Collect your information.
- Now Navigate to the Developer tab.
- Click Insert
- Click on the Scroll Bar.
- Click anywhere on your worksheet using the Scroll Bar (Form Control) button. A Scroll Bar will be added to the worksheet as a result of this.

Thank you!

Thanks for reading this book.

If you appreciated this book, I would be extremely grateful if you would take 1 minute of your time to leave a review on Amazon about my work. You can use the QR code below.

If you didn't like it, I am very sorry. You can write me at **leonardwebbwriter@gmail.com** *to tell me how to improve it.*

Thank you.

Leonard Webb

SCAN THE QR CODE

WITH YOUR MOBILE

Customer reviews

★★★★★ 4.9 out of 5

44 global ratings

5 star		90%
4 star		10%
3 star		0%
2 star		0%
1 star		0%

˅ How are ratings calculated?

Conclusion

Microsoft Excel is a significant spreadsheet and data analyzing computer program with a broad range of capabilities. Different kinds of data can be organized, calculated and kept data saved for future use. Excel grid interface allows you to organize virtually any type of data you can think of. It is a powerful tool for performing analysis and what-if scenarios. To calculate the various circumstances, you employ formulas in a cell; make spreadsheets of your sales, charts for presenting your data.

In today's world, it has become an essential tool across the globe for many reasons. As excel is easy to use and an ability to add and remove information without causing any difficulty, MS Excel is frequently utilized for a wide range of tasks. When it comes to anything involving financial activity, Excel is a need. Making new spreadsheets with bespoke formulae for everything from a basic quarterly forecast to an entire corporate annual report makes Excel enticing for many people.

Excel is popular for organizing and monitoring common information like sales leads, project progress reports, contact lists, and billing. Finally, Excel comes in handy when working with huge datasets in science and statistics. Using Excel statistical formulae and graphing features, researchers may more easily do variance analysis and visualize large amounts of data. Microsoft Excel plays a vital role in so many industries. In the following departments, the importance of Microsoft Excel may be observed.

In this book, we have learned everything about Microsoft Excel, the Introduction of Microsoft excel, its history, its versions. We learned about its inference and Ribbon. The commands and buttons we can use to make our work easy from different tabs of the Ribbon. We learned to enter, edit, modify, sort, filter, and validate data. Concept of worksheet, cells, columns and rows. Everything about Excel formulas and functions in the easiest way possible is being explained in this book. Difference between functions and formulas and how to use them. Shortcuts for excel that can make you work fast and be done with it within minutes. Shortcuts are also being sorted according to your ease like there are shortcuts for editing, shortcuts for excel overall.

This book is your ultimate guide for Excel and will help you learn and work on Excel easily without any complications. This book is an accessible guide for day-to-day use and may help you learn this program in no time, whether you are a student, working, or retired.

TUTORIAL: How to Create Family Monthly Budget Using Excel

Budgeting in Excel or financial management allows you to keep track of your money, such as expenditure and income. To keep a record of your monthly revenue and expenditures, you'll need a budget planner. It will also assist you in spending the appropriate expenditure items at the appropriate proportions when you are in debt or financial hardship.

A budget is a forecast of revenue or income and spending or cost for a certain period. The budget planner examines your spending patterns. There are several Excel templates accessible, but it is always preferable to create your own. The directions below will help you how to create a monthly budget in Excel.

Step 1

Prepare a table and fill in the row and column headings as seen in the screenshot.

	A	B	C	D	E	F	G	H	I	J	K	L	M	N
1	Budget													
2		Jan	Feb	Mar	Apr	May	Jun	Jul	Aug	Sep	Oct	Nov	Dec	Year
3	Income													
4	Salary													
5	Interest/Dividents													
6	Others													
7	Total													
8														
9	Expenses													
10	Mortgage or Rent													
11	Car													
12	Phone													
13	Health Insurance													
14	Food													
15	Others													
16	Total													
17														
18	Short/Extra													

Step 2

Enter your revenue and spending budget data into the table, then compute the total incomes for each month and item:

(1) Estimate your total monthly earnings. In Cell B7, type =SUM (B4:B6), then drag it to apply it to the whole Range from C7 to M7.

(2) Analyze each item's total income. To apply this formula, type =SUM (B4:M4) in Cell N4, then extend the Load Handle to the whole Range N5:N6.

(3) To add up the total income for the year, use =IF (SUM (N4:N6)=SUM (B7:M7), SUM (N4:N6), FALSE) to fill Cell N7 and hit Enter.

Step 3

Evaluate the total cost of every month's spending as well as the cost of individual items.

(1) Insert =SUM (B10: B15) in Cell B16 to add up all of your monthly spendings, then drag it to apply the equation across the whole Range C16 to M16.

(2) Insert =SUM (B10: M10) in Cell N10 to determine the cost of each item, then slide to use the equation to the whole Range N11 to N15.

(3) For Cell N16, enter =IF (SUM (B16:M16)=SUM (N10:N15), SUM (N10:N15), FALSE) to calculate the overall cost for the whole year.

Step 4

Use a pie chart for the revenue for your budget year.

(1) Choose Range N4 to N6 by pressing down the Ctrl key, then use Range from A4:A6.

(2) Click the Pie icon on the Insert tab to choose a pie chart from the drop-down list.

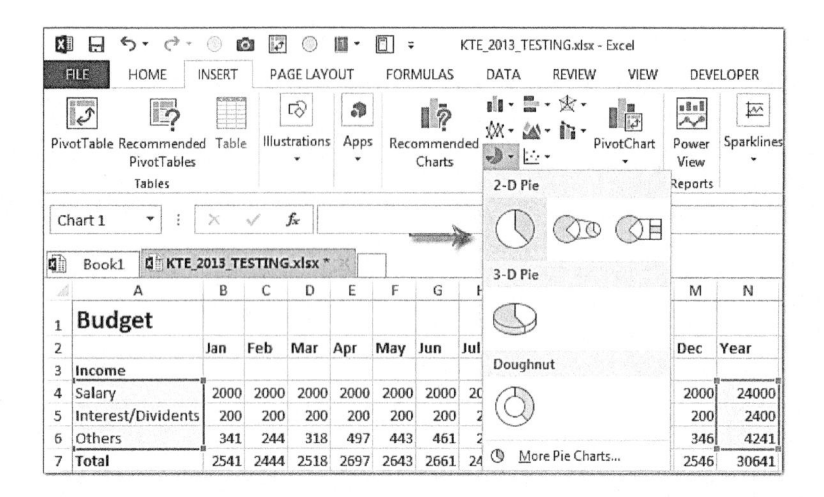

Step 5

Format the new pie chart that has been inserted.

(1) Right-click the pie and choose Add Tags from the right-click menu to add labels to the pie chart.

(2) Click the Layout, then click the Chart Title to add a title to the chart. Title of the graph

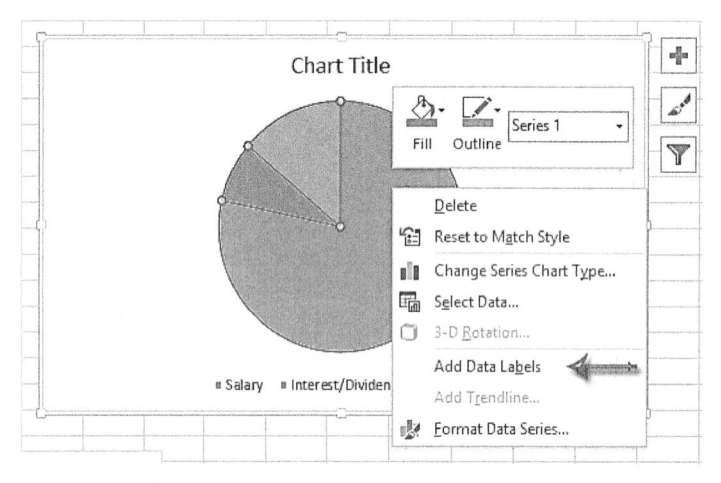

Step 6

Include a pie chart for this budget year's spending.

Please pick the A10 to A15, then click the Ctrl key and choose the N10 to N15; then use the same ways as in Steps 4-(2) and 5.

Step 7

Save the current worksheet as a template by choosing File, then Save, then Computer, and then Browse.

The current worksheet has been saved.

APPENDIX

50 MOST USEFUL KEYBOARD SHORTCUTS

Action	Shortcut
Close a spreadsheet.	Ctrl + W
Open a spreadsheet.	Ctrl + O
Save a spreadsheet.	Ctrl + S
Copy.	Ctrl + C
Paste.	Ctrl + V
Undo.	Ctrl + Z
Cut.	Ctrl + X
Delete column.	Alt + H,D, then C
Go to Formula tab.	Alt + M
Go to Home tab.	Alt + H

Navigate in cells

Action	Shortcut
Move one cell to the right in a worksheet. Or, in a protected worksheet, move between unlocked cells.	Tab
Move to the last cell on a worksheet, to the lowest used row of the rightmost used column.	Ctrl + End
Move to the beginning of a worksheet.	Ctrl + Home
Move to the next sheet in a workbook.	Ctrl + Page Down
Move to the previous sheet in a workbook.	Ctrl + Page Up
Move to the edge of the current data region in a worksheet.	Ctrl + Arrow Key
Extend the selection of cells to the last used cell on the worksheet (lower-right corner).	Ctrl + Shift + End
Move one screen up in a worksheet.	Page Up
Move one screen down in a worksheet.	Page Down
Move one screen to the right in a worksheet.	Alt + Page Down
Move one screen to the left in a worksheet.	Alt + Page Up
Move to the previous cell in a worksheet or the previous option in a dialog box.	Shift + Tab

Format in cells

Action	Shortcut
Format a cell by opening the Format Cells dialog box.	Ctrl + 1
Add or edit a cell Note.	Shift + F2
Display the Create Table dialog box.	Ctrl + L or Ctrl + T
Enter the current time.	Ctrl + Shift + Colon (:)
Switch between displaying cell values or formulas in the worksheet.	Ctrl + Grave accent (`)
Use the Fill Down command to copy the contents and format of the topmost cell of a selected range into the cells below.	Ctrl + D
Apply the Percentage format with no decimal places.	Ctrl + Shift + Percent (%)
Apply the Date format with the day, month, and year.	Ctrl + Shift + Number sign (#)
Apply the Number format with two decimal places, thousands separator, and minus sign (-) for negative values.	Ctrl + Shift + Exclamation point (!)
Check spelling in the active worksheet or selected range.	F7
Edit the active cell and put the insertion point at the end of its contents.	F2
Open the Insert dialog box to insert blank cells.	Ctrl + Shift + Plus (+)
Open the Delete dialog box to delete selected cells.	Ctrl + Minus (-)
Enter the current date.	Ctrl + Semi-colon (;)
Open the Paste Special dialog box.	Ctrl + Alt + V
Use the Fill Right command to copy the contents and format of the leftmost cell of a selected range into the cells to the right.	Ctrl + R
Apply the Scientific number format with two decimal places.	Ctrl + Shift + Caret (^)
Apply the Time format with the hour and minute, and AM or PM.	Ctrl + Shift + At sign (@)
Create or edit a hyperlink.	Ctrl + K
Display the Quick Analysis options for selected cells that contain data.	Ctrl + Q

Make selections and perform actions

Action	Shortcut
Select the entire worksheet.	Ctrl + A or Ctrl + Shift + Spacebar
Start a new line in the same cell.	Alt + Enter
Select an entire column in a worksheet.	Ctrl + Spacebar
Repeat the last command or action.	Ctrl + Y
Extend the selection of cells by one cell.	Shift + Arrow Key
Fill the selected cell range with the current entry.	Ctrl + Enter
Select an entire row in a worksheet.	Shift + Spacebar
Undo the last action.	Ctrl + Z

Printed in Great Britain
by Amazon